Beyond the Paddle

Beyond the Paddle

A Canoeist's Guide to Expedition Skills—Poling, Lining, Portaging, and Maneuvering Through Ice.

Garrett Conover

Tilbury House, Publishers
Gardiner, Maine

Tilbury House, Publishers
The Boston Building
132 Water Street
Gardiner, Maine 04345

Library of Congress Catalog Card Number 90-071661
ISBN 0-88448-066-6

Portions of this book first appeared in *WoodenBoat*
Cover and text designed on Crummett Mountain by Edith Allard
Copyediting by Liz Pierson, South Harpswell, Maine
Editorial assistance by Janice Brackett, Gardiner, Maine
Layout by Nina Medina, Basil Hill Graphics, Coopers Mills, Maine
Imagesetting by High Resolutions, Inc., Camden, Maine
Printing and binding in the United States of America by Arcata Graphics, Kingsport, Tennessee
FIRST EDITION
Cover photograph by Alexandra Conover
All text photographs by Garrett Conover, except where he appears. In those cases, photographs are by Alexandra Conover.
All drawings by Garrett Conover, except for chapter openers. These are by Jerry Stelmok.

For E. O. C. and W. B. C.

Contents

Acknowledgements

In drafting these words I realize that *acknowledgements* also serve to trace my addiction to the wild places and the heritage that surround the techniques of travel and passage to wilderness.

My father mixed his interests wonderfully, and balancing his engineering side was an interest and some ability in art. Before I could read I was swept away by the paintings of Charles Russell, Frank Schoonover, and others who had a sense of accuracy and a love of wild land. My mother was a naturalist and encouraged my explorations even as I broke the rules and undoubtedly endangered myself any time I could explore a little farther than my parents may have intended. And while citing parental contributions, their greatest gift, in addition to being themselves, was to raise their children in the absence of television and with an abundance of books. To that I owe my imagination.

Family friends Pat and Don Kienholz have always had a canoe or two to enhance their wilder wanderings and that detail was never lost on me. By age thirteen, at a camp in Vermont, I was finally given skills and a strict standard of perfection for which to strive. That we boys used aluminum canoes did not slow the learning, and that the camp director Bob Easton had a scratchless wood and canvas canoe that no one save himself could approach revealed a higher standard to which to aspire.

There are the authors and artists, far too numerous to list, of canoeing literature, history, natural history, exploration, ethnography, and wilderness skills who paved my way through all levels of school and college until such time as my addiction could be steered to the various masters available, and more tangible and immediate exchange could take place.

Mick and Eunice Fahey deserve far more credit and gratitude than can easily be stated. They allowed for an extended apprenticeship and grand friendship, and seemed willingly to suffer the countless questions an eager youngster could spill. And not just for me, but a half dozen others lucky enough to study the arts of the north Maine woods with such masters of craft and knowledge.

Two other grand masters have joined Mick on the far side of the last portage—Omer Stringer and Bill Mason. Although our meetings were infrequent and few, my gratitude and indebtedness remains large.

Many colleagues in the canoeing world must also be mentioned. Friends and neighbors Jerry Stelmok and Rollin Thurlow are the primary voices in the world of wooden canoes and share their knowledge and expertise with tireless enthusiasm. George and Linda Luste, Michael and Geoffrey Peake, Hugh Stewart, Craig MacDonald, Stewart Coffin, Harry Rock, and John Fradley Monroe have all increased my knowledge of northern canoeing in countless ways and with great detail.

For bridging the gulf between current recreational canoeing and the last days of canoeing for life and economy a special thanks to Eleanor Wheeler, Elliott Merrick, and Horace Goudie.

Our own apprentices Jane Barron, Dave Lewis, and David Mussey deserve thanks not only for their excellence in the field, but also for their role in carrying on the traditions of the Maine Guide. Along these lines, although not a registered guide, Kimberly Kafka has paddled and snowshoed in Maine and Labrador, and with the other apprentices appears in several of the photographs here. Also thanks to Cindy Pearse and Nancy Sosman, Kevin Budd, Tom Allen, Ginny Bouchard, Matthew Heintz, and Mike Shannon who appear in some photographs. And Just Black and White photo lab for processing work.

For refining our teaching abilities and levels of inquiry by asking great questions, the many participants on ten years of North Woods Ways trips and courses are heartily thanked. The many people who made up the audiences of various lecture halls and who would always think of something that would send me scrambling through the archives and libraries for answers are likewise thanked.

Not to be overlooked is my dearest partner of the paddle and snowshoe trails, and indeed of life, Alexandra Conover, who shares and reciprocates my passion for northern heritage and skills.

Everyone must join me in thanking copyeditor Liz Pierson who with patience and exasperated humor slogged through my original draft, converting the ramblings of someone who writes by ear and invents punctuation and syntax into something sensible and familiar to those with a grasp of grammar and proper usage. Were it not for her consummate skill, I would be destined to perpetual embarrassment and you to eternal befuddlement.

In conclusion, I must return to the mention of my late father, Bill. We are both hilariously noncompetitive, and this trait set the stage for our "fiercely competitive race" to the publisher. To an observer there would be precious little evidence to suggest anything as dramatic as a "race," and they would be hard-pressed to point out any cut-throat tactics, but Bill and I enjoyed the idea mostly because it made us grin. It was also a bit of a catalyst for our brand of achievement. He sold some paintings, I published an article; eventually he published a cartoon, and the years went by. Occasionally we would goad each other by saying, "Hey, you oughta send that in." We both had the idea of books, and perhaps having something to say, in the back of our minds. We never knew what or when or if, but the seeds were there. With the unfair advantage of his absence (although he once introduced a clause that would allow him to change the rules of the race at any time to enable him to "win"), I have now sent one in. I wish he were here to see the result, for we were always so proud of each other.

Introduction

There comes a time in a wilderness canoeist's career when a strictly downriver trip is no longer enough. Perhaps it is not wild enough or removed enough or too many fly-in parties are populating the route. Perhaps one is retracing a trade route or planning a multimonth or multiyear trip where a single watershed is simply not long enough. The traveler may have learned that many of the significant wildlife encounters are often on high ground and that the spiritual elements of living, however briefly, in some portion of the shrinking wilderness require a remoteness not easily accessible along the major routes of canoe country. Whatever the combination of events and feelings that inevitably take hold of such a canoeist, the first symptoms are likely to show up during the excitement that arises when reviewing the maps of their next big trip.

Slowly at first, but with increasing persistence, the thinner blue lines of the river systems become attractive and the blank spaces between watersheds are studied for narrow spots, preferably low, perhaps with a few small ponds here and there to shorten some of the portaging. The phrase *I wonder* becomes a refrain as the route planner gets thoroughly and willingly lost in patterns and

Beyond the paddle is another realm where tools, techniques, and attitudes may grace the traveler's ways and spirit.

dreams. *I wonder where this leads, or where it comes from, or what might this watershed hold? I wonder if I crossed here, went upstream there, crossed this height of land and descended this unnamed stream until it rejoins...*

And so dreams take shape, build in excitement, and soon become full-fledged plans where before there was only quiet musing over topographers' symbols.

The accuracy of modern maps made possible by satellite surveys, sophisticated photography, and computer-enhanced resolution of natural systems has left little in the way of the unknown for the wilderness navigator. Still, there are areas to be explored, and maps don't know or tell everything. Terra incognita may be lacking, but personal and spiritual explorations are still very much the domain of oneself and one's chosen companions. The maps no longer contain true white space where the lay of things is unknown; but where the blue lines of the waterways get thin, where shorelines and bays are intricate, and where the spaces between watersheds are just right, the world again becomes large. Little-traveled areas do exist, and plenty of canoe country is large enough to lose oneself in.

Beyond the Paddle is not a key to dreams, nor does it suggest what routes might be good. It is a key to technique and expertise that will allow the imaginative to go where they will with grace and fluency. It is an introduction to the skills of travel that have been refined over time—traditions of canoe usage that have settled with sophisticated elegance at their present state of evolution. *Beyond the Paddle* deals specifically with the nonpaddling skills that any serious wilderness canoeist should constantly be honing, the skills that will gain one access to the remotest regions, the skills that will increase one's possibilities and pleasures and ease one's passage to that wildest country.

The wilderness canoeist by inclination and preferred habitat has chosen to specialize in the branch of canoeing that has the most to gain from a traditional approach. While our contemporaries may be specializing in the narrower-focus disciplines of speed paddling, white water, or solo or tandem ballet, the traveler must become expert in a wide range of skills—must become a Renaissance person of the canoe. The reasons are evident in and arise from the landscape itself.

Since being peopled after the retreat of the last ice sheet, those regions of North America that have become known as canoe country have inspired and favored refinement of the travel technologies of those who lived there. The solutions to nomadic life in the boreal north could yield little else but superbly elegant canoes and equally elegant snowshoes and toboggans. Ten thousand years is a long time in which to perfect the techniques and equipment best suited to northern travel. Many refinements have been discovered in such a long span of time, and the rigorous evolutionary editing of what does not work has left modern recreational nomads with an intact body of knowledge from which to draw inspiration as well as the means to hone their own traveling abilities.

Beyond paddling, there are skills handed down from our wilderness forebears that can greatly enhance our mobility and the level of grace with which we traverse the northern reaches of canoe country. There is no doubt that upstream travel, portaging, or lining up or down difficult rapids is work. Yet such work can be and, when done well, is rewarding and pleasurable.

Wilderness travelers have long observed that the most memorable portions of a journey are the most demanding and often require the most judgment and technical finesse. The feelings of accomplishment and self-reliance and the joys of gaining remote vantage in a special land have ever been more than reward enough for the work inherent in the process of achievement.

Beyond the Paddle is a handbook for introducing efficiency and economy of means to those whose explorations will frequently rely on the nonpaddle aspects of canoe travel.

There are scores of books and articles on the finer points of paddling technique, and some are very good. Many more are poorly written and do little but rehash what is available in the better sources. Virtually no skills book, however, covers the nonpaddling aspects of canoeing with sufficient depth, and most make no mention of such topics. Those that do may introduce readers to the existence of a skill but leave them high and dry when it comes to imparting any technique or wisdom. A few are actively discouraging. One author advises that poling may be fine for Indians and Maine Guides but is so complex and difficult to master that the average canoeist need not be troubled by attempting to learn. It is a far greater disservice to mention such skills without follow-through than to leave these topics alone. None of these skills can be learned by trial and error with any effectiveness, yet this is what will be done in the absence of a mentor and in the presence of a little, but not enough, information.

Beyond the Paddle eliminates this void in the literature of canoeing. It covers the arts of poling, portaging, lining, tracking, and using the ice hook with sufficient detail so that readers can begin to practice and refine these skills with thoroughness and safety. The reward will be the ability to apply one's growing expertise in the context of remote sojourn.

Mastering these skills will not eliminate the hard sections of a given trip but, by reducing the strain and disheartening elements of struggling without knowledge, it will vastly increase the grace with which one can travel. It will also yield a tremendous energy savings, which will increase the pleasure of the experience as a whole, as well as retain that reserve for all the special pleasures of the trail that lure us into the wilds in the first place. After all, there are flowers to see, side trips to take, and the hope of encountering wolves or musk-oxen, moose or caribou. Chances are there will be sunsets or the aurora borealis to watch, watercolors or sketches to be made, photographs to be taken, or archaeological sites to be found. There may be some splendid fishing to be sampled or bird or geology guides to be put to use. May such gifts be part of all our travels.

Beyond the Paddle

1

The Northwoods Canoe

Before applying the paddles and other forms of locomotion to a canoe, before loading it with gear, and even before selecting the hull for use or purchase, it is wise to understand the demands that will be put on the craft and what features will best accommodate the diverse needs of the long-term traveler.

This process can be confusing and fraught with difficult compromises. In addition to your personal balancing act are the limitations reflected in the market for expedition equipment, including canoes. Since the late 1980s, the trend among canoe companies has been increasingly toward specialization that leaves canoes with such a narrow range of function that those seeking a wilderness craft are now forced to use hull types that are so generalized that they perform nothing well, despite their wide range of potential. Anything with high volume and more than 17 feet in length tends to get lumped into the wilderness-tripper category of most manufacturers' specification sheets. There is more to a wilderness hull than length and volume, but precious few manufacturers are making any real effort to acknowledge refinements.

In understanding the features for a hull of the traveler's choice, you are immediately confronted with trying to balance a number of conflicting points. The fine entry lines that enhance paddling ease become a liability when applied to poling and white water. The appropriate sheer line for keeping rough water out of the canoe in the heavy stuff provides a large "sail" area for contrary winds to catch. The longer lengths that allow for ease of poling, refinement of lines, and improved buoyancy contribute to increased weight and provide for an unwieldy craft in tight rapids or during a portage through thick brush.

A hypothetically perfect traveler's canoe exists in the minds of a good many people. Yet in the marketplace not many canoes fulfill this hypothesis, and all of us are forced to make compromises, given the limited selection.

Ideally, the features common to traveling hulls will be these. The canoe will be symmetrical in hull configuration as well as sheer line. This enhances predictability in up- and downstream functions and allows for an up- or downstream orientation by design or mishap even in heavy rapids. In slower-than-current maneuvers, such as backpaddling, snubbing on a pole, or braking with tracking lines, ease of handling prevails with a symmetrical hull. Likewise, a symmetrical sheer yielding the same bow and stern heights improves your abilities in the same situations. Canoes with asymmetrical hulls and sheer lines that are different at bow and stern are specifically oriented for downstream travel under power and remain of limited use to the wilderness traveler.

Length will probably settle in the $17\frac{1}{2}$-, $18\frac{1}{2}$-, and in some areas 20-foot range. This is long enough to allow for fairly fine entry lines for ease of paddling yet retain a smooth flaring to fullness for poling, lining, and encountering the rough water of lakes and rapids.

The sheer will rise from the center-thwart area evenly to a height at the ends of 23 to 25 inches. This ensures a dry canoe in the roughest water that remains navigable. You will hear plenty of arguments that this much sail area presented to the wind is going to be a real problem. To the unskilled it can be a serious problem. But to those who learn to paddle well and trim the canoe appropriately for each given wind, the trade-off is entirely satisfactory. It has always struck me as odd that despite the pervasiveness of the wind argument, the last canoes off the water in deteriorating conditions are those with rising sheer lines that keep the waves in the lake rather than in the canoe. Far earlier in the escalation of wind-bound conditions, the more wind-resistant canoes with their lower sheer have wisely made it to shore or have swamped in the process of ascertaining conditions. In waves that are not induced by wind but are produced in the rapids, a rising sheer is a complete advantage.

The hull shape of the best traveling canoes will show a shallow arch to the bottom, flared sides in the ends to shed waves, and straight sides amidships, or at most just a hint of tumblehome—enough to enhance side strength by the slight arch but not enough to encourage shipping waves. The end profile of travel hulls is not as critical as that of a strictly white-water canoe or flat-water racer, but nothing extreme will show up. Most will show a tendency toward being plumb or only slightly recurved or flared. The fanciful extreme recurve on some canoes may be aesthetically appealing to some but does little for the functioning of the hull.

Since the traveling hull will be subject to white water in the context of lining, poling, and paddling, it will have a fair amount of rocker fore and aft, at least a few inches, though nothing as extreme as a white-water sport canoe. It

A fleet of E. M. Whites showing sheer lines.

will not have a keel or even a shoe keel as these are distinct liabilities in white water. Good paddlers can keep any canoe on course, even a highly rockered white-water canoe. The actual improvement in tracking ability provided by a keel in flat water is minimal—and more a psychological aid than a real one. The only significant thing that can be observed in keeled canoes is that if they are wood and canvas and used carelessly, the canvas near the keel is usually in better shape than the fully exposed canvas elsewhere. It is far more sensible to become skilled at paddling and canoe care and dispense with keels altogether.

The above characteristics reveal a canoe that is a specialist at accommodating a wide range of functions in potentially rigorous conditions. The compromises made for such contrary needs as white water and flat water, upstream and downstream directions of travel, faster- or slower-than-current maneuvers, the needs of portaging in all terrain types, and the choice of characteristics that favor poling and paddling functions are all achievable through subjective balancing that considers each individual's expertise and abilities within the context of their canoeing landscape. The far more daunting elements in achieving hypothetical perfection are the limits within the marketplace and the selection that is available.

Here again there is a complete range of options. In synthetic canoes, the most commonly seen choice in the wilds is a tripping canoe made of ABS (Acrylonitrile-Butadiene-Styrene), which is impact but not very abrasion resistant, heavy, full enough in the ends to be buoyant, but paddles poorly, doesn't pole, and has a hull that "oil-cans" even with a load in it. The only things in its favor are that it is very dry because of depth and volume and can manage a big load for longer trips. These last two attributes are enough for a good many wilderness travelers to choose such a canoe and are regarded as adequate balance for the far more numerous negative aspects.

Compared to the great number of materials available in the synthetic world of canoes, the more refined end of the scale is represented by four different canoes that are made in wood and canvas. The 17-foot Chestnut Prospector, though boxy, unfair, and relatively hard-chined, is revered as a fine wilderness

Loaded canoe in waves on Moose River.

canoe all across the Canadian north. Despite its lack of aesthetic lines, it is a workhorse of remarkable prowess under all conditions. Two other historic canoes that are still available are the 20-foot and 18$\frac{1}{2}$-foot E. M. White canoes. Both are remarkably close to perfection for their intended wilderness roles. The fourth member of this fleet of superb canoes is a new design. The Atkinson Traveler is a 17$\frac{1}{2}$-foot canoe that blends the best features of the two E. M. White models into a remarkable wilderness canoe of grace and function. All of these canoes are available in limited numbers from craftspeople committed to the best of traditional and current possibilities. Although the Chestnut company suffered a long, tortuous demise during which time quality was not a high priority in either materials or workmanship, those builders now working from Chestnut or Chestnut-style forms are producing fine canoes, many of which are far superior to the products of the original company.

Although not an available option for most of us, there is another, more extreme, approach to the notion of perfection. Renowned northern canoeist Stewart Coffin of Massachusetts didn't find anything that met his exacting specifications. So he learned how to work with Kevlar and other materials and manufactured his own hull, which he likes pretty well, though each trip inspires more tinkering and adjusting. His evolving hull is so satisfactory that each year several people commission him to make a canoe.

Within this range of possibilities will be a canoe or canoes that in the end are acceptable enough to select. Each of us will find our particular level of compromise and accept the limitations that are part of the bargain. My choices have settled around the E. M. Whites and the Atkinson Traveler, which are represented in most of the pictures in this book. In the end, the choice will blend material preferences, weight, expense, acceptable design limitations, and a web of compromises. The trick is to apply as much informed reasoning as you can to an otherwise subjective choice.

Once you have selected a hull, there is one final refinement you can make that will make your traveling life infinitely easier. Trimming your canoe for different aspects of travel or to accommodate winds or current will make all

Descending Chase rapids on the Allagash.

elements of travel more pleasurable and convenient. A tradition that has long been part of the working canoe culture of Maine is a waterline running the full length of the hull. On wood and canvas craft the line is achieved by the interface of paint above and orange shellac below. The orange shellac provides an easily maintained bottom finish that is slippery on underwater obstructions such as rocks and logs and on ice.

The waterline is a reference point and not a true waterline. Aesthetically, a line struck halfway between the rail at center-thwart and the bottom of the canoe and carried to the ends on the level is the best looking and the easiest to see. With the exception of extreme loading of the canoe, it will be visible and therefore offer ready reference to your trim.

Following chapters will discuss trim for specific applications in detail. For general purposes, however, the following guidelines are usually true. For flat water with no wind, a level trim is best. For a head wind that allows forward progress, a very slight bow-heavy trim will ease your passage. For a following wind, a very slight stern-heavy trim is best. For ascending a current, a bow-light trim is essential; for running a rapid downstream, where slower-than-current maneuvers such as ferrying and backpaddling will take place, a slight bow-heavy trim. For poling and lining functions, an extreme upstream-end-light and downstream-end-heavy trim are essential regardless of the direction of travel relative to the current. In all cases, the dominant forces, whether wind or current, are used to "weather-vane" the canoe, allowing the paddlers to concentrate

Rivière à L'Eau Claire Labrador.

on forward and in some cases lateral progression with economy of means.

By shifting gear or people, proper trim can be achieved. Despite the enormous benefits that proper trim yields, most canoeists know very little about the topic. Since most people unwittingly trim bow-light no matter what they are doing, a lot of unnecessary work and aggravation are endured and many hard feelings and lapses in group and paddling-partner dynamics are created.

Anyone who strikes a waterline on their canoe before it ever gets near the water will be rewarded many times over by the benefits of readily referenced trim. Be it shellac, paint, a stripe of tape, or a spiffy self-adhesive pinstripe from an automobile accessory store, a waterline will soon be regarded as essential equipment. You will in fact remain puzzled that it was ever possible to get along without one.

With canoe selected and waterline in place, it is time to gather up gear and depart for the wilds. There you will learn the subtleties of the canoe and discover the limits of what hull and personal expertise can accomplish given the conditions encountered.

The high dry carry around Holeb Falls on the Moose River.

Late season travelers gain solid safe ice by paddle and ice hook in a water-lined Atkinson Traveler.

2

The Art of Poling a Canoe

Harvey Goudie and Ralph Blake are the best team on the pole and it's as good as a hockey game to watch them do a bad place. Both stand half crouched in the canoe, their poles swinging together like clockwork. Each throws his whole weight into the shove as though there were never any such thing as a pole slipping or breaking. The canoe surges ahead, never veering an inch, stops while the poles swing in unison, surges ahead again, as though by magic.
True North by Elliott Merrick -1933

If you scan the various areas of canoe country that contain gently dropping rivers, or trace the trade routes that once made use of rivers that weren't so gentle, chances are you will find a history of poling. In a few areas you may even find a few individuals practicing and skilled at the art.

A revival in poling is occurring in a limited way as a result of competitive events focusing attention on the skill. And though competition generally involves speed and finesse skills in empty canoes, such events have roots in the historical context of poling and the practicalities of travel and commerce.

Wherever canoes needed to traverse water that was too shallow for effective paddling, you once found polers. Propulsion opportunities could be maximized in shallow, calm water, and the descent and ascent of shallow rapids was not only possible but extraordinarily effective.

For the wilderness traveler, the skill of poling remains, in its pure form, a practical matter that increases efficiency, reduces wear and tear on equipment, enhances the traveler's level of control and safety, and in extreme cases makes passage possible where others must line or portage.

Road proliferation, the advent of the outboard motor, and the coming of bush aircraft all contributed to the general disuse of poling skills. Anyone involved with work upon the waterways was quick to invest in alternative transportation strategies. Ironically, it was the guides and rivermen who adopted the outboard motor and made motor brackets for their canoes who kept poling alive until canoe recreationists seeking a wilderness experience found a new application for the skills of self-propulsion.

Lumbermen and guides retained their poles even as they perfected their river-running skills with outboard motors. Just as they had formerly protected their paddles in the shallows by poling, they redirected the skill to protect the shearpins and props on their outboards. But even so, the additional power supplied by motors made ascents and descents of white water possible in deeper and stronger sections of the river, and slowly the feats of the best polers were no longer being matched.

Fortunately, when the wilderness recreation boom began to gather momentum and canoeists began to seek wilder areas to avoid motors, fumes, noise, and the dependencies inherent in the use of fuel technologies, older people skilled in the ways of the rivers were still around to pass on the body of poling

Horace Goudie, one of the last active "Height O' Landers" of Labrador, poles an E. M. White up the Atikonak River.

knowledge. Although poling is still a rarity even on the waterways in the epicenter of poling traditions, a small but growing number of younger guides and travelers are rediscovering the pleasures of the art.

The areas where poling never died out, and where the skills associated with it reached their highest refinements, are in the Province of New Brunswick and the state of Maine. The reasons for this cultural quirk can be discerned in the landscape itself or from maps showing the drainage patterns and wealth of rivers.

The legendary Atlantic Salmon streams of New Brunswick are still home to the 20- and 22-foot canoes that draw so little water and can negotiate the shoals and bars between pools that fly fishermen travel far to sample. Guides with spruce setting poles and a lifetime of shallow water savvy can still be found. Outboard motors and neoprene waders have been added to the angler's tool kit but have not eclipsed the presence of poles or those who know how to wield them.

In Maine you find a land creased with the dendritic patterns of large and small waterways where distances between watersheds can be incredibly short. Although some stretches of water have remarkable pitches of unrunnable rapids, there are rivers where you can canoe 100 miles without a portage. Native Americans traversed this intricate interior, which was once as wild as Labrador. Trappers, lumberers, and others followed these well-worn trails, and now countless recreationists traverse some of the most historic routes.

The reason that Maine and New Brunswick waters were the seats of refined poling technique has to do with the rather gentle gradients of long river systems, the cobbly, bouldery nature of the riverbeds, and the seasonally different water levels. The long, shallow-draft canoes that are such good polers can often continue to navigate the much lower water of late summer and fall.

The fact that the carries were few and generally short favored the big 20-foot E. M. White canoes that poled so well, paddled beautifully, and had the volume and sheer to handle the white water of spring when the rivers run so high with melt water. With only a handful of carries over a mile or two long, and these widely separated, the 90 to 100 pounds of a 20-footer were a bargain to the woodsmen of Maine.

To learn poling from those who did it best and maintained the tradition the longest is a rare opportunity. It is also a gift that can be applied anywhere in canoe country where the rapids get shallow or where the current in an ascent is too strong to paddle against.

Traditionally, poles were made by the users, often at stream edge with an axe and crooked knife. Among the native people, who were known to refrain from carrying extra baggage, a good many poles were discarded or put to different uses as a trip progressed. For most of us, however, a good pole becomes part of our permanent traveling equipment and is given the same care and respect as a fine paddle.

For the traveler, a spruce pole is still the best. It is light, warmer than the synthetics in spring and late fall, of a diameter that is easy to grasp when poling loads, and easy to make if you have access to a table saw, a few good planes, and a source of good clear spruce. Some of the wood and canvas canoe builders also offer poles for sale. And of course you can still make them at stream edge, as the need arises, with an axe and crooked knife.

With the renewed interest in competitive poling, Mad River Canoe of Waitsfield, Vermont, has been selling aluminum poles for a few years, and there is a company that sells a fiberglass pole, which unfortunately is far too flexible to be effective for poling a loaded canoe.

In days past, iron pole shoes were cast by companies that made tools for loggers and those who worked the woods. This is no longer the case, and those who have a few of these old-style pole shoes guard them jealously. They are cone-shaped and tapered to a blunt point that can find purchase on most underwater surfaces, including smooth ledges. Their weight is such that a pole in the water will float, yet when the pole is held up, the shod tip sinks quickly to the bottom even in the fairly strong water of rapids. Poles with too light a shoe have to be pushed to the bottom, and in strong water this extra element of concentration and activity is always annoying; in a tight spot, it can use seconds that could be critical for other needs.

The more commonly seen solution to shoeing wooden poles is to put a ring of copper pipe at the bottom to prevent the end from "brooming" and splitting. Many people screw a large lag bolt into the end and hacksaw the nut off the top, leaving an inch of spike protruding. As the spike wears down with use, it can be backed out with a pair of vise grips. This is effective until the threaded section tapers too much for the hole to hold firmly, at which point a new bolt can be inserted after the other is removed.

The optimum length for a pole is 11 feet. When not in use it is stored with the top end under the stern seat and tucked as far into the stern as it will go. The rest of the pole lies along the rail with the shod tip just outboard, ready to be dropped into the water quickly when needed. A longer pole will interfere with the the bow person's paddling, unless you take the trouble to switch the pole to the opposite side of the bow person every time they switch paddling sides.

Effective poling occurs only in water less than 3 feet deep, and extra length is not generally needed by the poler working topside.

Of equal importance to pole placement is the position of your paddle during poling. It should always be placed within easy reach yet secure enough so that it will not slip overboard. A little practice should allow you to ship your

Getting Started: Acquiring a Pole

Different pole shoes clockwise from top left: traditional cast shoe, copper ring with lag-bolt spike, copper ring only, trimmed bare wood, broomed bare wood in need of trim, unshod aluminum, and final two aluminum poles show a Delrin plastic plug with spikes. Last pole is of a diameter favored by racers.

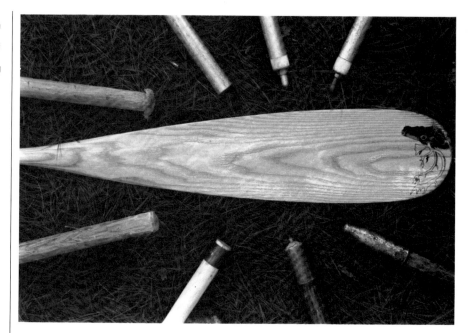

Pole placement when pole is not in use.

paddle with one hand as you draw the pole into a useful position with the other. Likewise, you should learn to ship the pole while picking up the paddle. This economy of movement and timing can be important in a tight spot such as when your pole gets jammed and you must release it. In this case paddle control is better than no control.

Making a Spruce Pole

Finding clear spruce in long lengths is getting increasingly difficult as the overall quality of our forests deteriorates. Still, the occasional clear piece shows up. If you live near a lumberyard that is friendly enough to let you pick over the stacks, a good place to start is in the 2 x 6 rack if they carry 12-foot or longer planks. What you need to find is a plank so clear that somewhere in it you can locate a knotfree section that runs the full length and is at least $1\frac{1}{2}$ inches wide. Should you find such a piece, or one that contains several poles worth of such wood, you are in luck.

Once you get the plank home, you need to saw it out on a table saw. After you have reached one edge of the clear section in which your pole is, set the saw so that the piece you cut for pole stock is as wide as the plank is thick. The result will be a square piece, and this will simplify your job of liberating the pole from this square.

At this point you have to make a decision. Will this be a pole that you use from only one end or from both ends? If it is to be end-specific, you will want to taper the pole over its length. If it is to be spun end over end or if you will switch ends as you switch sides, you will not want to taper it.

Let's suppose you have decided that your pole will taper and be shod at one end only. With a compass, inscribe a $1\frac{3}{8}$-inch circle on the bottom end and a $1\frac{1}{8}$-inch circle on the top. If your source stock was planed lumber, it will be about $1\frac{1}{2}$ inches square and the larger circle will nearly fill the end.

Since each piece of wood will flex differently, it is best to remove wood slowly, which gives you the option of taking off more if you need to. Removing too much at the outset leaves you no option. Clamp the pole stock along the edge of a long workbench. Using the longest plane you have, plane each corner off the square the full length of the pole at a 45-degree angle to each original surface. This will yield an octagonal pole. If each face of the octagon is of equal width and the edges are parallel, you have a perfectly straight pole that is centered in the wood you started with. Any discontinuity in width indicates that you are not centered; lines that

are not parallel indicate a curve introduced by not planing all sides equally.

During this process work lightly and evenly on all sides. Check the ends periodically so you don't remove too much wood for the minimum diameters that you marked with the compass.

Once you have a nice octagonal piece, test it for flex. It should have rigid spring but still be able to bend a bit. If it is wobbly and already too flexible, abandon the piece and seek a different plank to start from. If it is too stiff and unyielding, you can slowly and evenly remove more wood—but maintain an equal octagon for a cross section. Once you have reached your minimum-size lines, the pole should be close to proper flex. Your frequent flex tests, however, will be a better guide than specific measurements. Some poles will need to be a little larger in diameter, and some will allow you to plane beyond the compass lines.

Assuming all has gone well, you have a fine springy octagon that requires no further thinning at the large end. If you have not already done so during initial planing, it is time to add the taper that runs toward the top. The smaller circle you drew at that end with the compass will be the guide. Plane each face of the octagon with long even strokes until you reach this circle. The start of this taper is not necessarily at the very base of the pole but may start about 4 feet back from the large end.

Here another choice gets made. Many polers leave the bottom 4 or 5 feet octagonal. This may be more rigid than a perfectly round pole when a strong current passes the pole. It also looks nice. Above this point, or any point you choose, the pole is round in cross section.

After you have tapered the top end in its octagonal form, you can make it sixteen-sided by planing off the remaining corners. This process continues to yield reference lines for checking to see if the pole is true and centered. If all lines are parallel and equidistant from each other, you are all set. If the flex is good, your pole is nearly done. The sixteen-sided part is so close to round that coarse sandpaper will finish the job on that end; if you have chosen to leave the bottom section octagonal, sanding after folding your sandpaper around a sanding block will keep your lines parallel and the faces between them flat and flush. As a further refinement you may wish to plane the transition zone lightly from round to octagonal a few feet in either direction to fair the taper out a little. Or you could work this section a little harder with coarse grit sandpaper. Start with 60- and finish with 120-grit.

If you plan to use a copper-pipe-and-lag-bolt shoe, select an outside pipe diameter that is smaller than the diameter of the pole. A 3- or 4-inch section of copper pipe will yield enough weight to sink that end of the pole well, especially if the walls of the pipe are fairly thick. To prepare the pole for seating the pipe, cut in equally on all sides with a saw or chisel and remove enough wood for a cylindrical cross section so that the pipe fits snuggly. If you need to drive the pipe section on with another block of wood, the snugness is just right. Before driving the pipe section on, make a 1-inch-deep saw kerf so that the end can accept a wedge after the pipe is fitted. Another way of doing this is to initiate a split with a chisel after the pipe is on. A softwood wedge driven in should secure things perfectly. Saw any remaining pole and wedge that protrude beyond the bottom of the pipe, leaving only a $1/_8$–inch of wood beyond the edge of the copper.

If a lag bolt is going to be inserted, drill an appropriately sized hole to accept the screw, insert it, and saw off the head leaving an inch or two of the shank exposed as a spike. You can then either file the tip blunt or let the river bottom wear it smooth. Fair the wood above the pipe section so that it meets the edge of the copper smoothly. With no edges to catch between underwater rocks, your pole will not get stuck so easily. If you file a bevel on the bottom edge of the pipe section, you will have a smooth, clean-lined shoe. You will repeat this filing over time as the copper is soft enough to blossom out a bit with the constant banging it receives through use. This bit of maintenance could be required as often as once or twice a season, or more if use is frequent.

As a finishing touch you can shellac the bottom section of the pole with orange shellac for protection. Although you might oil the upper pole, it is best left unfinished unless, like oil, the finish penetrates rather than coats. Bare or linseed-oiled wood is much easier to grab with maximum friction than is a varnished or painted surface. In fact, when the going gets really strenuous you will often see polers reaching down and dipping their whole pole in the water because a wet pole yields even more friction for power transfer.

If you plan to shoe both ends of your pole, make the entire pole round in cross section and don't taper it. To keep things as light as possible, a shorter ring of pipe at each end provides the best shoeing arrangement.

If clear lumber is not accessible but a spruce woods is, you may choose to make your pole from a standing dead spruce sapling. Choose a young spruce for straightness and a diameter that is not much bigger than your finished pole will be. If you will be making the pole in a shop with access to planes and other tools, you will first want to square the pole and then proceed as outlined above. Working from the square yields constant reference to keeping things true, straight, and centered.

If you are in the bush and are making a temporary pole, you can cut one very close to finished diameter and at least trim the branches flush and carefully. If it is done in camp with some time available, you might want to make a better pole with a bit more care, and here again working from a squared piece will guarantee precision. An unshod pole made in the bush is very quiet on stream bottoms and useful for approaching wildlife closely. Every so often the broomed end can be trimmed with a knife as wear and tear on an unshod pole occur rapidly.

Any time temporary poles are made and used, it is best to lean them in a tree for others to use either as poles or firewood or for other campsite uses. Those that are abandoned carelessly to wash away in the spring high water, or that molder into the forest floor, reveal a more wasteful and discourteous traveler. When you encounter such stashes of material in remote country, there is the joy of communication with other unmet sojourners. Not infrequently, such caches provide a service when bad weather, inconvenience, or even emergencies befall travelers in need.

Once you have secured a pole, it is time to take your canoe to a shallow section of a pond or lake where no current will influence your initial familiarization process. At this point, accept on faith that a canoe less than 17 feet will not pole as well as one that is longer. The reasons for this will be outlined in greater detail later. You may discover the stability related elements on your own as you learn to break the cardinal rule espoused by most camps and canoe-use manuals: never stand up in a canoe. As an accomplished traveler, you will be standing up with increased frequency—to pole, for certain paddling functions, and as your skills improve, in some surprisingly choppy white water.

A windless day and water a foot or less deep will be perfect for initial experimentation. Since flat water with no current will be your medium, a flat trim or a slightly bow-light trim will be good. For this you can stand just aft of the center thwart and enjoy maximum stability as this will be near the widest part of the canoe. Weather and water should be warm enough for the discovery of limits, and you should dress for immersion.

Unlike competitors, who stand square to the canoe and use both ends of the pole equally by switching sides like a kayak paddler, you will be learning to pole from one side or the other, generally using only one end of the pole. Switching sides for more than one or two corrective jabs will involve a change of stance.

For the traveling poler, your feet should be spread both side to side and fore and aft. This diagonal positioning lines up your body for the most effective use of leverage and musculature for nontiring yet powerful poling. At the same time,

Left

Forward thrusts should be performed parallel to direction of travel for optimum power and directional integrity.

Right

Descending a rapid with a loose, relaxed, yet responsive stance with knees slightly sprung to absorb canoe motion or impact.

the fore and aft positioning of the feet allows you to absorb any shocks, such as hitting a rock you didn't see, that would otherwise cause you to pitch forward or backward.

With your feet spread laterally as well, you can also absorb any shocks that might unbalance you from the side. This position also allows you to lean the canoe to either side or to apply torque by twisting your hips and torso. In combination with slightly sprung knees, this position leaves you perpetually ready to absorb surprises as well as to deliver maximum power to all your moves.

Initially the best exercise is to hold your pole like a balance bar and get used to shifting your weight and position around in the canoe. Start this process gingerly, and gradually explore the limits—up to and including jumping or falling out at the threshold of no return. During this process the canoe will tell you some things about your position in it, and your body will tell you some things about how much more fun it is to stay limber and loose in a plumb orientation to the center of the earth. At about the time that you can move forward and backward over thwarts without looking down at them, and can rock the canoe to the rail on each side with complete confidence, you are ready to start doing something with that pole you brought along.

There are two tendencies you will consciously have to fight while learning to pole. Don't bring the pole forward like a paddle off to the side for your next thrust, and don't plant the pole ahead of yourself when the propulsion you desire must be exerted behind you.

In the pole's lateral orientation, you must keep it as close to plumb and as close to the rail as you can. Distance from the rail only introduces torque, which you want only when initiating a turn. With your low hand on the pole, lift it forward parallel to the line of travel with a slight snap of the wrist while keeping the top of the pole forward and the shod end rearward. When the tip sinks to the bottom behind you, a thrust will instantly transfer power into forward motion of the canoe. If the pole tip is next to you, or worse yet ahead of you, you will have to wait until momentum has carried the canoe beyond the pole before you can apply thrust.

If you imagine a large clock superimposed upon your poling activity with your hips being the center, the three o'clock position toward the bow, and the nine o'clock position toward the stern, you can visualize some angles that will help you. Your forward direction of travel is the horizon beyond the three o'clock position. The angle your pole should never pass as you set it each time for a forward thrust will fall between the one and two o'clock positions for the top end, and the seven and eight o'clock positions for the shod end. This angle is 45 degrees from horizontal.

Power applied at any angle greater than 45 degrees is not productive; power applied at a lesser angle is increasingly productive until you reach the threshold where the bottom substrate no longer holds the pole. The hypothetical ideal for going forward is to push off a vertical wall directly behind you. Since nature will provide only a horizontal substrate below you, a compromise must be made and a pole angle somewhere between 30 and 45 degrees is the range for optimum thrust.

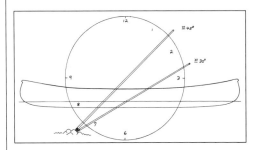

Now that you are scooting through the shallows with visions of clocks in your head, you are in a position to notice two things. One is beneficial and the other is frustrating. The beneficial aspect is that the faster you go, the more

While the stern poler shows a more typical 45˚ angle of thrust, the bow poler is taking advantage of a secure pole plant for increased power at something close to a 30˚ angle of thrust.

stable the canoe becomes. This results from dynamic stability, which is provided by the speed of the water passing the hull and providing a cradle for it to occupy. You can still tip over, but to do so you have to break the flow that is going fore and aft and introduce some motion that is 90 degrees to that. At a standstill, not much lean is required to break the inertia of the canoe at float. At speed, where the canoe is at float plus in a cradle of moving water, a more vigorous discontinuity is required to overpower the dynamic stability.

The frustrating aspect is that you are probably veering to your off-side, much as beginning paddlers do before learning to compensate. Remaining straight involves remembering to keep that pole close to the rail and nearly plumb. This maximizes the potential for keeping the line of force as close to parallel to the direction of travel as possible. This alone will not work because your push-point is off to the side of the centerline of the canoe. You can compensate by using your upper hand entirely for locomotion power and your lower hand both to push forward and to draw or push very slightly to maintain directional integrity. This will only work within a narrow arc, more than a few degrees of prevention or correction is not possible. This action will add some torque, which can be transferred through your feet with a subtle twist through the hips. This will prevent the bow from veering. Simultaneously, you can aim the canoe a degree or two toward the side you are poling on rather than straight ahead. The combination of all these factors and some practice eventually will come together, and you will be surprised at how fast you can go with complete directional integrity. As your skill improves, so will your sensitivity to nuances and fine points, which to a viewer will look more like body english than physics.

To initiate turns, push the stern laterally from the side. If you are poling on the right and you want to turn to the right, push the stern toward your left. In effect you will sideslip the stern around in a wider arc than the bow will travel. If you are poling on the right and wanted to turn to the left, you need to switch sides to push the stern toward the right. In poling, all forces are directed away from the canoe in the form of a push. This is true with forward power, lateral movement, and in applying the brakes by snubbing. In this regard poling is the opposite of lining. With the flexible lines, nothing can be done except under tension by pulling; with a rigid pole, all must be done by pushing as there is extremely limited potential for pulling a canoe toward the pole.

Once you can back up, go forward, sweep around turns, spin the canoe at will, and wander around in the canoe to shift your trim, it is time to head for some shallow moving water and learn grace and fluency in a current.

By the time you are ready to increase your knowledge of the intricacies of moving water, you will have become familiar with the weight and balance of your pole, its flex and strength, and a number of elements regarding stance and balance. Although the forces of a current will do much to oppose your efforts, they will also provide you with some predictability and, in many cases, assist you in poling. Your river-reading skills will be reinforced, and this ability will be transferable to paddling and lining in the rapids.

Initially select a mild current with few obstructions and just enough force to push the canoe around—but not enough to overpower you. Whereas the lake required a trim that tended toward flat, a current necessitates a radical trim that is peculiar only to poling and lining. Fortunately one simple rule covers all situations: The upstream end of the canoe must be raised so it is tangent to or slightly above the surface of the water. The downstream end will be correspondingly deep. This trim remains constant whether you are traveling upstream or downstream. This is the only trim that will allow poling to occur at all; anything else will be completely problematical and a curse.

A canoe thus trimmed is held in line with the current by the current itself. The upstream end presents no surface for the current to catch as the water passes beneath the canoe, whereas the deep downstream end is subject to the full force. In this way the water pressure itself swings the canoe to the angle of least resistance, which is parallel to the flow.

It is best to learn upstream travel first. The canoe's movement will be slower and its behavior more readily sensible regarding cause and effect. In an empty canoe, proper trim is easily achieved just by your own weight as you will probably be standing just ahead of the stern quarter-thwart. In fact, if your rearward

Ascending shallow rapid with a load positioned for proper trim. Note upstream end is free of current.

Radical trim for poling and lining. Regardless of the direction of travel, the downstream end of the canoe must be deep and the upstream end light enough so the stem is tangent to or out of the water. In the top figure a canoe is being snubbed downstream. The bow person, position of load, and the poler having moved forward all contribute to the bow being deep while the stern is high and light. In the lower figure the canoeist is going upstream. Again the downstream end of the canoe is deep but in this case it is the stern rather than the bow. The poler has chosen a position as far aft as is possible and absence of the bow partner yields a favorable trim without the need to shift the load.

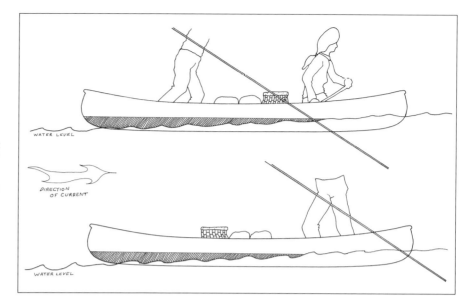

Coaxing a load up rapids that paddlers could never hope to ascend.

calf is braced against this thwart, you will increase your stability dramatically.

Basic river hydrology will tell you that the slowest water is the shallowest water near the edges of the river in a straight section and on the inside elbows of the curves. Here the friction provided by the riverbed slows the current the most. The deeper channels will have the fastest water because they have the least contact with resistance.

To stand still in a current, you will need to equal the speed of the water. To make headway, you will have to exceed it. In going upstream you are climbing a hill—and the steeper the hill, the greater the power and speed of the oncoming flow.

A very mild current will stop paddlers dead in their tracks. The medium a paddle uses for resistance to apply forward power is itself moving away from the canoe. A poler, however, reaches through the flowing medium of the water and uses the stationary riverbed for applying sufficient power to overcome the surge of the current. By staying close to shore and out of the fastest water, a poler can ascend some remarkably powerful rivers. If there are rocks and shoreline disruptions, then there will be eddies that actually carry the voyager upstream.

You need only look to the brawling rivers that tumble from the Labrador plateau, where many a downriver paddler gets feeling smug about their white-water prowess, to be humbled by the knowledge that countless generations of native people and the early traders ascended all those rivers by pole and tracking line. Some of these rivers drop close to 2,000 feet in 150 miles, revealing just how remarkable the potential for upstream travel is.

But before setting your sights on an ascent of the Moisie on the Quebec North Shore, let's return to that stretch of mild current in some open gravel-bottomed shallows. The basics learned here will provide the foundation for all the poling you do, including the most extreme applications you become capable of as your expertise grows.

With proper trim and the skills of balance and stance perfected in flat water, a mild current should pose no problems. In the shallows near shore you can probably ascend the stream with enough speed to make you grin. It is also time to experiment with crossing the current at varying angles. If you are familiar with the upstream ferry as a paddler, you will recognize the effect of sidewash on the canoe as a poler. Depending on your angle of set to the flow, the current will effectively move you laterally away from the surge. If the current is very mild, you may be able to go in any direction you point the canoe; if it is moderately strong, you may have to ferry side to side; and if it is a bit stronger than it should be for beginning practice, you may already have been spun around by the current despite proper trim.

Assuming you have had quite a bit of fun and have experimented enough with going upstream, it is a good time to turn around and see what a mild current is like in descending. With a completely empty canoe it will be inconvenient to trim just by moving forward. You will need to get just ahead of the center thwart to get the bow deep, and this will put you in a position where the canoe will still widen out toward the midsection behind you, as well as present a lot of light stern to any breezes that conspire to frustrate you. In such a mild current, however, you can probably descend at a rate faster than the flow and in fact aim the canoe where you wish to go. Since you will be exceeding the speed of the current, it will not act upon the canoe the way it would in stronger water where you would be working by ferrying. With speed, the extreme downstream-heavy trim is not essential.

When the mild-current practice becomes redundant, progress to a stronger section of the stream and perhaps a section with some rocks, corners, cobble bars, or other obstructions. If you have a friend along, you can both take short practice sessions to keep the frustration level low, and each can help with critique and act as movable ballast for proper trim. In the stronger water, trim will be more critical, and in learning to snub going downstream, it will become essential.

Again, start practice by ascending the stream. Your partner should sit facing the stern between the center thwart and the bow quarter-thwart of the canoe. Your weight in the stern, with one leg braced against the stern seat, should achieve proper trim. Your partner is in a comfortable position to observe and learn, and you can switch positions as fatigue or frustration dictate.

Despite being in stronger water, you still may be able to overpower the

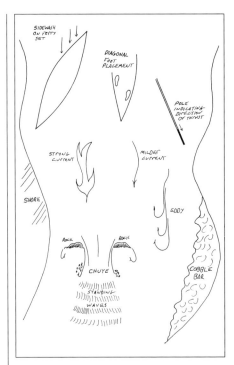

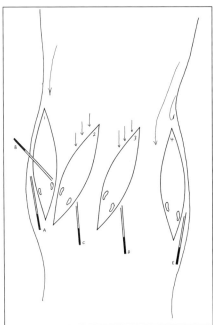

Upstream ferry from left to right bank.

A. Pole holds canoe in place along shore.
B. Pole pushes bow out to establish set for the ferry and at the same time the poler repositions feet to pole on the downstream side of the canoe (C & D), while maintaining the proper set for the sidewash to move the canoe toward the right bank.
E. Pole holds canoe along bank in eddy, ready to continue ascending.

current and go where you want to by brute force. This will not teach you very much that is useful except how strong you are and how much stamina you have. This is good to know—but not nearly as important as learning technique and the finer points of saving energy. After applying a certain level of brute force, bullish people will get tuckered out enough to pay attention to details.

After entering the current with your observer comfortably leaning against the bow quarter-thwart, two things become readily apparent. The canoe is vastly more stable with the load, and it of course draws more water, which increases what marine folks refer to as the "wetted surface." The increased stability is a nice gift, but the increased weight means that the poler must work harder. Not only is there more weight, but the increased draft and wetted surface provide greater friction on the hull. In going upstream not only are you pushing the weight of the canoe, yourself, and your load up an inclined plane, but that inclined plane is moving toward you like a conveyor belt and applying friction to the canoe. Upstream progress will exist only where you can overcome these forces, and at some point a threshold exists where diminishing returns on effort inspire you to get out the tracking lines or portage.

Common sense suggests that you will want to find the shallowest water that will permit passage, as this will be the least forceful and therefore the easiest to overcome. If you pole on the side of the canoe that is closest to shore and angle the bow just a degree or two toward that shore, the current will hold your position fairly well and allow you to spend most of your energy on forward

Upstream in an open current.

Ferrying from side to side to favor the inside of curves where there is calmer water, and changing stance as necessary. Bow person is walking up river yielding proper trim without repositioning the load.
A. Ascends stream to head of the calm water near shore.
B. Sets stern left to present the left side of the canoe to the current to engage sidewash and initiate a ferry to the right across the main current.
C. Ascends river just to the right of the main flow and at a slight angle to it so the current itself will hold the canoe away from the strongest surge.
D. Between canoes 3 and 4 the poler shifts stance to favor power on the left and downstream side of the canoe, while ferrying across the main current to stay in the less forceful water on the inside of the curve. The direction of the canoe remains constant here because the curve in the river provides for a proper ferry set thereby saving the poler from the need to establish the angle.

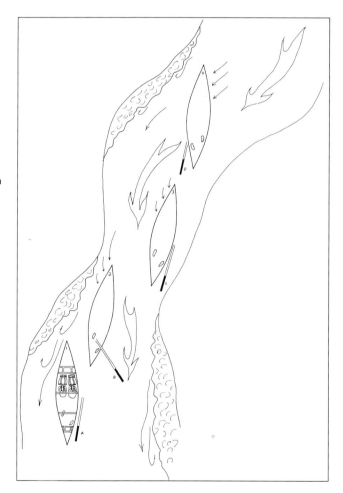

progress. At corners and places where you need to get around something, you will break out of full forward orientation and invest varying levels of force into lateral movements until you realign for straightaway power.

In water with rocks that break the surface and a shoreline full of irregularities, you will find plenty of eddies in which the water is actually going upstream. Use these whenever they present themselves. These little rests will keep you relaxed and ready for short bursts of power and speed for breaking out of eddies back into the current and for surmounting low chutes where the water is temporarily more powerful.

As the water pressure increases, you will find that your range of controllable alignment within the current decreases. In the mild water you may have been able to cross the current nearly broadside without losing much ground. Now you will find that an angle of 45 degrees to the current is all you can control. Beyond that the current will spin the bow no matter how you are trimmed. As the water power increases, this angle decreases until even the slightest misalignment will spin the bow downstream and thwart your intentions.

These angles are not only useful as thresholds of control but also reveal the set or angle to the flow most appropriate for ferrying either right or left.

Suppose you have come up below a big rock by getting into the eddy below it and now need to get a few feet further toward midstream in order to pass between rocks a little further upstream. The water coming off the rock you are behind is strong, and you know that with the stern in the upstream circulating eddy, and the bow in the main rush of river, you will spin and lose your position. And in a rocky stream you may not have room to spin without broaching on other rocks. If you back out of the eddy and initially set the stern into the current, the worst that can happen is that the current will push you back into the eddy. If you can overpower it, you can sideslip out into the current and then present a very small ferrying angle for the current to catch, which will assist your lateral movement. As the poler, you will maintain lateral alignment for the set of ferry to function as well as supply enough forward power to gain ground until ready for realignment and further ascent.

Initially you will want to practice crossing eddy lines and current differentials with a clear space below you that is large enough to allow the canoe a full 180-degree uncontrolled swing. As your confidence grows and your recovery skills evolve into preventative skills, you can push your skills into tighter confines.

After taking turns ascending, you can begin to practice snubbing down a stream. The movable ballast provided by your passenger will now move right up into the bow area ahead of the bow seat, and if desired, face backward again in order to watch technique.

In the stern you will step forward and either straddle the rear quarter-thwart or at least brace your forward shin on it. This will lift the stern out of the water in compliance with the rule of trim that requires the upstream end of the canoe to be tangent to or out of the water.

This shift of trim can be done along the shore with the canoe still facing upstream. This will allow you to practice a deliberate about-face, letting the current do all the hard work. The first step is to get close along the shore in an area that is open for twice the length of the canoe. Retrim for downstream travel and then sideslip out a few feet away from the shore. The poler can then let the

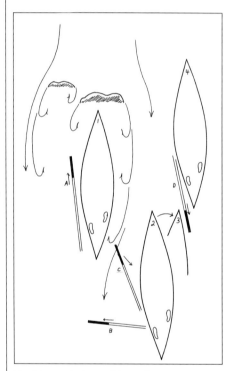

Backing out of an eddy and sideslipping to a new approach.

Reverse poling A backs canoe to the tail of the eddy. Pole thrusts B and C sideslip the canoe to the right for a slight ferry angle and further current assists slip toward the right. Thrust D initiates continued ascent up the river. An attempt to exit the eddy too close to the rock would most likely result in spinning the canoe 180 degrees as the current would catch the bow while the eddy would influence the stern in a way that would assist a spin.

bow out into the stronger downstream current toward midstream, and the power of the river will swing the canoe for free. If you hold the stern in position with the pole or actually push it upstream, the speed of this process will be increased.

With the current aiding rather than opposing progress, your first concern will be to control the speed of descent. This is done by snubbing with the pole and checking speed by lightly and repeatedly applying the brakes. Where poling forward requires the pole to be at an angle behind you, snubbing requires that it be well forward of you when it encounters the stream bottom. Again, keeping the pole close to and parallel to the direction of travel is best for all but initiating lateral movements.

In mild water, you can stop the canoe with a single pole-plant forward while absorbing the shock with your arms. However, as water power or the canoe's momentum increase, you will need to apply a series of snubs that slowly bring the canoe to a desired speed or, if need be, a complete stop. Very often you will need to alternate sides in snubbing to keep the canoe in proper alignment parallel to the current. In mild water you can usually safely cross-body pole, in which case you shift sides with the pole diagonally across the canoe in front of you. This is a very compromising position to be caught in should the pole tip get stuck between rocks; because of this, cross-body poling should be done selectively and kept to a minimum.

When you do get caught—and you will—try to limbo under the pole before it knocks you out of the canoe. Some remarkable gyrations have been done by people in this predicament, and sometimes recovery has been successful. Ideally the pole should be parallel to the rail on the side of the canoe being poled on. In this way a pole that gets stuck can simply be released without danger of unbalancing either the poler or the canoe and load.

In snubbing downstream, the techniques reveal a less visible cause-and-effect relationship. Expect a bit of dyslexia and a temporary inability to recognize right and left. Your eyes will deliver messages to your brain as usual, but poling technique in going downstream requires a mental reversal of approach. Suddenly you find yourself in a vehicle with the steering mechanism in the back. Like the steerer on the rear wheels of a hook-and-ladder fire truck, the poler now seems to be doing everything exactly opposite of what you would expect. This can unnerve your bow partner.

Suppose you casually announce to your bow partner that you will be going left of the next upcoming rock. That may be true, but the first impression a forward-facing bow person gets is just the opposite. It is all a matter of perspective and which end of the canoe you occupy. As the poler in the stern, you know that to cause the current to ferry the canoe to the left, you must push the stern left to set up the appropriate angle for the ferry to take place. The bow, of course, feels like they have just been pointed off to the right even though they heard you say left. That initial impression is correct; to go left during a downstream ferry, the bow does point off to the right because it is the sidewash on the right side of the canoe that pushes it and the load to the left. All this occurs because the descent is slower than the current. The ferries are engaged for changing direction because the current does all the work for you that way. The river is going downhill anyway; it won't get tired, and it is nothing short of a reward for exquisite laziness to successfully make it do the work.

Although perceptions may be confusing, the physics are simple. It may be that you have approached the start of a shallow rapid and have switched from paddle to pole. A few gentle snubbing motions break the momentum and slow the canoe while you look over the possibilities. At first things are quite open and easy and you can aim where you are going and get there because you can go under power and therefore faster than the current. A little way down, the current gets more forceful as the gradient steepens. Here the brakes go on again, and the canoe is let down slowly with frequent switching of sides to keep in line with the current. Where the water spreads out through a fan of boulders, there are multiple channels to choose from—but none are aligned and successful passage will require a lot of zigzagging between rocks.

Alternating sides to fine-tune alignment in small chute. Off-side snubs, left top and left bottom, are calculated risks.

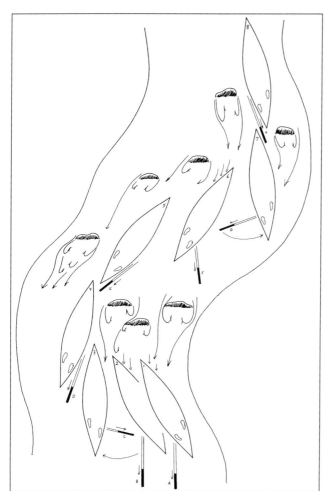

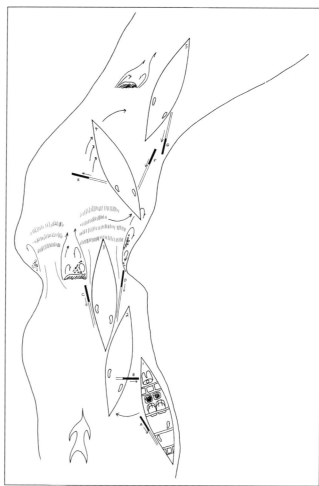

Left: S curve through rocks with ferry left, and right, showing side and stance shifts.

A and B ferry canoe toward left around the first reef of rocks and poler shifts stance in anticipation of next move. C sets stern behind bow for new alignment for ascent D and E which is straight up the current lines in short clear section. F establishes a slight ferry angle for current to ferry canoe right. G lines up stern with bow while stance is changed for continued ascent H.

Right: Snubbing down through chute and ferry right.

Note bow person kneeling ahead of bow seat for proper downstream trim. In addition the stern person poling has stepped forward to increase downstream-heavy trim.
Pole plant A holds canoe in small calm spot while strategy is planned. A shift of stance and pole plant B ferries the canoe into line with chute. Snubs C and D fine tune position and snub C was a calculated cross-body snub where the stance was not changed. After dropping through chute, E sets stern into eddy on right, while snub F stops momentum and drift so the sidewash swings bow in line and avoids rock. Again pole plant E was a calculated risk across the body without a change of stance. G is a straight ahead push into open water.

Suppose your first move requires that the canoe sideslip to the left. After applying enough brakes so the canoe is nearly stopped relative to the current, you push the stern 3 or 4 feet to the left. With the right side of the canoe now catching the surge of the current, it will move toward the left. Meanwhile you have switched to the left side and snubbed straight down the stream, stopping the drift of the canoe. The current instantly swings the bow in line with the stern, and the canoe is now parallel to the current and some 4 to 6 feet farther left of where it was. If this new position is not far enough left, you can repeat the process until the canoe swings in line with the channel you need for continued passage.

This braking, ferrying, and swinging into line is basically the whole foundation for descending on a pole. If you enter a cul-de-sac, you can simply turn around in the stern and pole your way back upstream until you can try another route. As you descend you will find that part of the time you will go faster than the current and therefore can aim where you are going; or there will be stretches where you can drift at current speed until such times as you need to slow down to ferry to one side or the other; and in the heaviest stuff that remains navigable on a pole you will be snubbing for all you are worth and progressing quite slowly, but not as slowly as lining or portaging would be.

Two things that you should be ever vigilant for while descending a rapid on a pole are (1) getting your pole caught between rocks and (2) the current getting so strong that you can no longer slow down and stop in it. In the case of the latter, you have lost control and the current that was formerly cooperating in moving your load is now endangering you and your equipment.

So far you have suffered a lot of words to understand the rudiments of poling. By way of review you can dispense with that and look again at the schematic diagrams of routes through the hypothetical poling situations.

Applied Poling

When the need for poling arises on a trip, not much will be different from what you may have experienced during practice sessions—except that the overall weight of the load will have grown significantly with the addition of a full camping outfit. In going upstream you will find that a fairly mild rapid will be much more difficult than it was in an empty canoe or when carrying only one passenger.

If the shoreline or riverbank is fairly open and easy to walk through, the bow person can walk while the stern person does the poling. Not only does this remove a significant load from the canoe, but proper upstream poling trim is achieved automatically without shifting the load.

There are of course areas where the riverbank will not provide easy going, and in such a place you may opt for tandem poling, which will require a shift in gear placement to trim properly, or you might resort to lining the canoe up the river. It may be that some gear can be portaged while the canoe is poled or lined. Explore all the possibilities and combinations and select whichever methods save the most energy and time.

Assuming that the terrain allows the bow person to walk, then ideal conditions have been encountered. If the poling stretch is fairly long, you can shift on and off and thereby gain a rest, or at least a change of pace.

With a loaded canoe you will quickly become skilled at using the eddies to help reduce your work load. Your route selection will most likely be an alternating series of ferries from side to side as you favor the inside of curves and eddies behind rocks. In between will be surges of current where you must go straight up against the flow. In these sections a direct approach is best as that is the angle of least resistance for the hull.

Over time you will know what you can overpower and what angles are possible for ferrying in various currents before encountering the threshold where the current will swing the bow out of your control. Likewise you will discover where you can simply power out of an eddy back into the current and where it would be prudent to back down near the tail of the eddy and sideslip into the current before presenting any angles for sidewash to catch. You will discover where it is best to take a long "pole-stroke" and perhaps climb the pole hand over hand and where it is all you can do to move forward with short little jabs of power during which the pole is not even taken all the way out of the water but moved ahead through the water so the current has no time to force you backward.

Although poling is ostensibly a means of maintaining control in the shallows and much of that involves the avoidance of rocks, you can learn to use the rocks almost as chocks to keep the canoe from losing ground. This can be done by easing the canoe alongside a rock and letting the current hold it there. You do not want to slide along rocks and abrade your canoe, but many times a tangential encounter that temporarily holds the canoe is useful. This is most often a possibility when crossing complicated diagonal currents that want to spin the bow. If a rock happens to be in a good spot, it can hold the bow in place while the poler sets up for the next thrust.

If you get in a tight spot in mild water, it is a simple matter just to step out of the canoe and wade it to a better area, or to step out and grab the rail if you are losing control. Riverbeds are not without surprises, and a few times a year polers find themselves falling. If possible, fall into the canoe. If you feel a full-fledged humiliating wipe-out coming on, do your best to make it dramatic or amusing or both for your companions.

Descending on a pole is generally easier and faster because the current is for the most part assisting you. At least it is going in the same direction, and gravity is an ally. In this case keep your bow partner in the canoe for trim as well as assistance. You may have to move the heaviest gear forward, but often you can trim properly by having the bow person kneel as far forward as they can, and you can stand forward also and perhaps straddle the stern quarter-thwart to get the bow down.

Your bow person can be of great assistance as a second pair of eyes, as someone who can help hold the bow in position either by paddle or a bow pole, and can generally make life easier for the standing poler in the stern.

Again, you may need to step out and grab the stern if you begin to lose control. Try to fall into the canoe if you fall, and remember that in descending you have the greatest potential to get your pole caught between rocks. Although you should keep cross-body poling to a minimum, you will find it convenient to do. As your poling skills improve, you will do more and more of it because you will become better at judging when and when not to risk doing it. With a bow person aboard, you will have to lift the pole over them when you switch sides. Getting whacked in the side of the head by a swinging pole is no fun for the victim and never improves your paddling relationships.

Remember if your pole gets stuck to let it go. This is not as easy to do as it might seem on paper. You keep thinking that maybe you can extract it, but meanwhile the current pushes you up on it or past it. It can knock you out of the canoe if it is a cross-body jam or flip you out if it is downstream and the

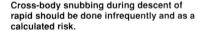
Cross-body snubbing during descent of rapid should be done infrequently and as a calculated risk.

canoe rides up on it broadside. In this case, if you don't let go, the pole will literally pull you past the point of no return regarding balance. It's very unfair—you can't pull the pole but it can pull you. So just let go.

Oftentimes a jammed pole will fall over and float down to you. But every so often one gets jammed very well and sticks up out of the river and throbs in the current. Rarely will a pole thus stuck do so in an accessible manner. I have a friend who fathered a Theory of Maximum Inconvenience based on this very problem. He observed that this only happens to the last canoe down a pitch, so that following craft can't retrieve the errant pole, and that it always happens in a place that is too strong to pole back up to and too deep to wade to. Or it happens when you are alone and it's November and shelf ice and cold water are all around complicating things.

Tandem poling offers an entirely new realm of possibilities and should not be overlooked. There are two methods, and both are very rewarding to those who use them.

The first method can be treated either as an end in itself, or if you plan on learning the second method, as a stage in the learning process. All the rules of trim apply, and all the techniques and intents remain the same. What is gained is an increase in power and a great deal of useful assistance from the bow.

The bow person wields a short pole, about 7 feet long and similarly shod if

Tandem Poling

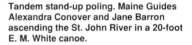

Tandem stand-up poling. Maine Guides Alexandra Conover and Jane Barron ascending the St. John River in a 20-foot E. M. White canoe.

it is a permanent pole. (Former full-length poles that have broken often become bow poles to increase their life span.) It is used from a kneeling position, which keeps the center of gravity low and improves overall stability. When straight-ahead forward power is being applied, both polers work from the same side of the canoe. Only when directional integrity demands it will the bow person temporarily switch sides. In tight spots, sides may be switched frequently to wiggle the canoe through a maze of rocks and, in snubbing downstream, sides may be changed as needed, but these changes occur when forward power is not great.

Generally both polers will pole simultaneously, but in ascending a rapid that is near the limits of possibility, the polers may shift to the off beat so that the canoe is never left unpropelled and at the mercy of the current.

If you wish to experience the full potential of the art of poling, you can try tandem stand-up poling where each of you has a full 11-foot pole. With both bow and stern polers, standing leverage and power are maximized and stronger water can be ascended or descended. Coordination, balance, cooperation, and communication are the primary ingredients of this activity, and the results never cease to amaze even those who become expert.

That tandem poling is not more common probably has to do with most people not bothering to carry so much duplicate equipment. Although it may be standard for one pole per canoe to be along on a trip, it is rare for others to be added. Single poles are problem enough on carries and when stowed, and if conditions merit tandem poling, most travelers will cut and make additional poles as needed rather than carry them.

Beyond the basics of poling outlined here are the things you must learn empirically. The rivers and canoe will teach you all the main ingredients. You will learn which rules cannot be broken, such as trim, and you will learn when and where other rules can be bent or temporarily broken.

Should you ever have the opportunity to watch or take part in competitive poling, it will increase your appreciation and understanding of the art. Being aware of or fluent in those differences between race poling and classic poling will increase your understanding of all aspects. Both the similarities and the differences in each activity are illuminating and revealing.

Perhaps more than any other nonpaddling aspect of canoe travel, poling cracks the door to a new dimension of discovery and joy. The problems of shallow water turn to intrigue, trip ideas expand upstream as well as downstream, horizons widen, and the kingdom we have been in all along suddenly has new features and possibilities.

Similar but Different: Poling for Travel or Sport

The basic premise is completely shared between competition poling and travel poling: the negotiation of shallow water and in particular shallow quick water. The physics of thrust, leverage, torque, and power all hold true, but there are some significant differences in approach. Most of these are goal related, and the differences in technique reflect this.

A more accurate term for competition-style poling might be sport poling. It is engaged in for fun and as an end in itself. The differences between it and travel poling are analogous to the differences between sport white-water paddlers and wilderness travelers who are skilled at white water. The sport paddler seeks the thrill of finesse in upperclass white water in an empty canoe designed solely for heavy rapids—and that most likely is filled with airbags, has a pedestal seat with thigh straps, and can be rolled like a kayak should the need arise or the paddler wish to practice for fun. The traveler, by comparison, may enjoy white water as fun and thrilling, but it is a smaller element in a larger picture. The practicalities of long-term travel with large loads require a more holistic as well as conservative approach. Such travel is fun for its practitioners but infinitely broader in scope.

The sport poler enjoys a similarly narrow and specialized focus and again is not encumbered with a load or any greater context than the activity of poling itself. The equipment evolves into a more specialized form, and techniques that may have had practical origins shift to accommodate the more esoteric needs of extreme application. Where a sport white-water paddler has gained the skills to negotiate the fringe limits of possibility, a traveling canoeist has long since taken to the portage trail. Where a traveling poler would avoid the worst water in a shallow rapid to protect the load and ease passage, the gate setters for a poling slalom would place the buoys in a way that forces the sport polers to demonstrate their skills in the heavy stuff.

Sport polers favor lighter and shorter canoes, which is possible due to no load. The aluminum poles they favor have a weight and flex similar to a spruce pole, but they are shod at both ends and can be wielded end over end and side to side like a kayak paddle, in addition to being used in the standard plant-and-push methods familiar to a traveler. Since sport polers work both sides of the canoe equally, they adopt a square stance and shift to a diagonal only during the steepest ascents where they pole on one side for some length of time and require the additional leverage provided by the diagonal.

In descending, sport polers generally proceed under power and as such are going faster than the current, which precludes the need to trim downstream-heavy. The speed requirements of the race course are achieved by forward power, not by going slow and allowing the current to do the work. With no load, there is no need to enlist the current. Where the traveler works at a steady, long-yield pace that makes use of the least forceful currents and eddies, a racer has no such choice where the course seeks out the difficult and extreme. Often the gate placement requires the poler to travel in the least sensible places. Virtuosity is the goal, and anyone who demonstrates the best speed under duress and difficulty shows the most highly developed skills. It is very exciting.

Although spruce poles are seldom used in competition, aluminum poles can be used in travel. Their weight and flex are nearly the same. The only drawbacks are that they are very cold in early and late season and have such a small diameter that snubbing a load down a tough rapid can be difficult for someone with large hands. It is much easier to hold the larger diameter spruce poles all day without cramping your hands under extreme loading or power application. Vinyl tape on the aluminum will make the pole a little bit warmer and will prevent your hands from becoming black with oxidized aluminum, which gets on everything else you touch.

Beyond that, you can decide if you want to use both ends of the pole or not. It is one thing in mid-August in a temperate climate to pole wind-mill style along one side, or to pole kayak style over alternate sides, but by September you won't enjoy being soaked when the water and air are cold. By November it won't be a decision at all; you will be doing everything in your power to keep things dry. A pole with the lower end sheathed in ice is bad enough, but allowing any splash that freezes on your clothing or that makes the canoe floor slippery is not to be encouraged. Better to pole carefully on one side only and leave the baton twirling for the showpeople of summer.

3

Handling the Lines

A crowd of jolly trappers we are leaving one and all.
The first trapper has started up to portage Muskrat Falls
And getting in our canoes boys, oh it seems so fine,
Heading up Grand River with our poles and tracking lines.
A Labrador Trippers Song

As a wilderness canoe traveler gains experience and begins to explore ever higher and farther along the watersheds of canoe country, it is probable that the use of tracking lines will become preferable, if not necessary. Through common usage, the term *tracking* refers to upstream work and *lining* to downstream work. In either case, tracking lines, or simply lines, are used to control the passage of canoe and load, usually from a position onshore or from the shallows and rocks near shore. The art of lining requires a thorough understanding of current, its friction on the canoe, and the ferrying behavior of a properly trimmed canoe in current. Everything must be done by tension or lack of tension. As liners repeatedly discover, you cannot push a rope.

As with other aspects of refined technique, lining is far more difficult and complicated than it might appear, and it is vastly more difficult than any of the schematic diagrams that illustrate it indicate. It is a skill that should be practiced and learned under gentle conditions with small loads. Like poling or whitewater paddling, it should be learned before a trip rather than on a trip as the need arises.

Under most conditions where lining is an option, navigation by canoe is already a marginal proposition. Lining occupies a very limited niche in the canoeist's repertoire of skills; it is the final possibility for avoiding a portage and is not without risk to canoe and equipment. As with navigating rapids by pole or paddle, lining is primarily a mental exercise, one of careful evaluation of conditions, strategy, and your level of expertise. You must know the limits of your canoe and yourself.

The strategy ingredient is not to be taken lightly. Include not only the planned line of progress but alternate routes that acknowledge retreat and recovery options should you need them. While pondering these points, play out all the worst-case possibilities. This tempers your enthusiasm and sharpens your ability to evaluate the situation. If any of the worst-case hypotheses leave you puzzled regarding a solution, that is your best clue to head for the portage. This is the same habit of caution that should infuse all aspects of careful canoeing. Then and only then should rehearsed and understood physical techniques be brought into play. Properly applied, the art of lining is as intriguing and exciting as any other aspect of travel and, where effective, it is a great energy saver and efficiency boost.

Before you arrive at the water's edge, there are two important things to consider: length of lines and location of line attachment.

Length is based on a few simple factors. Too much line can become a problem in terms of stowing it, keeping it tanglefree, and inhibiting ease of handling. Too little line reduces the maneuverability of the canoe and can lead to its own forms of disaster. It is far better to have more line than is generally needed than to wind up in a situation where you are at the end of your rope and need more slack.

Balancing between too much and too little must take into account how much line you can handle in open coils without entangling the line or your feet as you move along the shore or through the shallows. Twenty-five feet is long enough for introductory purposes and for many purposes is close to ideal. The more line you have out, the more difficult it becomes to control the canoe and load. Although experienced liners often take 45 or 50 feet, they rarely let the canoe go much beyond 30 feet. The remaining line is reserved for occasions when more slack is needed or when you need to throw a coil forward to the bow or a third person while still retaining tension until the helper has full control of the thrown coil.

Once you decide upon length, the location of attachment at the bow and stern is of critical importance. Most canoes do not come with an attachment point for tracking lines, and those that do generally have them near the top of the stems or on the deck itself (see Figure 1). These locations are the worst possible because they are the highest points on the canoe and therefore yield tremendous leverage, which works to overturn the canoe. When a strong current passes under the hull obliquely or from the side, the skin-drag or friction on the hull rolls the upstream rail toward the water. Should the rail go under, the canoe instantly fills. Lines attached at a high leverage position guarantee a swamping—the very thing liners are trying to avoid.

The ideal point for attaching lines is the very bottom of the hull a few feet from bow or stern (see Figure 2). The problem is that this is the portion of the craft that receives the most abrasion during mishaps in the shallows. The next best solution is to attach the lines just above the waterline on the stems (see Figure 3). This does not inhibit any paddling or poling functions and allows the lines to be attached full-time. This point represents the best balance in

1. Line too high
2. Best - crotched line
3. Good - drilled hole in synthetic canoe

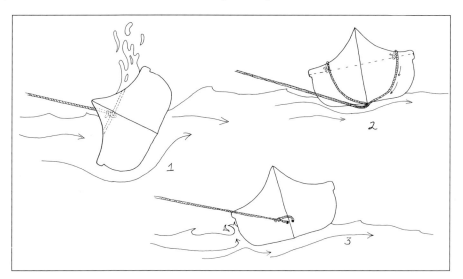

terms of being out of the way yet low enough on the stems to reduce significantly the leverage that works to flip the canoe.

The most specialized attachment makes use of a crotched line or bridle (see Figure 2). To create a 25-foot line in this case, you start with a 31-foot length of rope and an additional $6^1/_2$ feet of the same material. The rope must be braided in the three-strand twist format for a graceful *Y*, or side splice, which is done 6 feet back from one end of the long piece. The result is a 25-foot line with two 6-foot tails. The splice yields only a slight swelling where the joint is rather than a bulky knot, which would quickly abrade.

With a line of this type, the pull-point is at the best spot on the hull—dead center of the keel line on the bottom. This location nullifies the tendency of the canoe to roll toward oncoming current, and since the tails continue up each side of the canoe to the seat frames for attachment, the rolling tendency is countered by tension on the tail on the opposite side of the canoe from the person or people conducting the lining (see Figure 2).

There is, however, a price for this most effective of attachments: The lines are in a position to be abraded by rocks and ledges, and a certain amount of tying and untying may be required in stretches of river where lining is interrupted by sections of paddling or poling. For those who value the increased control, the inconvenience of periodically retying the lines is considered mild and even a bargain. If the canoe can be flipped by skin-drag with this arrangement in place, you should have been portaging all along.

You must make additional choices when selecting the material of the lines. Many safety manuals recommend plastic line in a high visibility color because it floats and is easier to see in rescue and recovery work. This is a good idea but more appropriate to white-water sport canoeists taking calculated risks in groups—most likely in warm water and weather, in nonremote settings, and with some or all members versed in rescue and extraction procedures.

For expedition lining, where much longer lengths are used, the plastics are totally exasperating. They are hard on the hands, twisty and kinky, and have very limited facility for lying well in open coils. The lower the temperature, the

Lining bridle showing end-splice at end of line, side-splice to create the "Y" in the bridle, and a whipped end for ease of knot tying when securing the bridle to canoe.

Bridle in place on canoe yielding a pull-point at or near center of hull on the bottom.

worse these factors become.

Many of the nylon ropes are available with a "soft hand," meaning they lie well, are pliable, and have a much reduced tendency to twist and tangle. They do not float, however, and depending on their quality they may stretch considerably under extreme loading (such as a swamped canoe in strong water). Despite this they are the most favored and are available in three-strand twist format for ease of splicing.

If splicing is not a consideration, any of the braided lines are fine, and there are other synthetics from which to choose. In any event, minimum stretch and a soft hand should be the primary criteria in choosing.

Natural-fiber line is not obsolete despite the flood of synthetics on the market. If you can find quality long-fiber hemp rope you will not be disappointed. Beware, however, of poor-quality shorter fiber ropes, for these are diabolically twisty, hard, rough, and awful in all respects. The good stuff is a different species altogether. It splices easily, lies well, does not break down in sunlight, and is not affected by temperature changes. It is easy to hold under pressure, has minimum stretch when wet or dry, and does not produce such serious rope burn should it slip through your hands suddenly. On the negative side, it does gain a bit of weight when wet and needs to be dried properly as it can mildew and rot when stored improperly.

The diameter of a lining rope must be thick enough so you can grab it without wrapping it around your wrist or hand. It must always be used by a free hand for controlled slip or, if necessary, complete release. Quarter-inch line is the smallest with which this is possible, and many prefer the slightly larger $5/_{16}$-inch line.

The conditions that make lining a useful strategy are generally related to rough water in which you might risk having a mishap, difficulty recovering spilled freight, or a swamped canoe. A more benevolent condition might be a runnable rapid that curves out of sight in a riverbed that is becoming so steep-walled that an en route pull-out or change of mind would be difficult or impossible if you proceeded too far. Lining is a way to save energy while retaining nearly complete control. This risk reduction makes any trip more relaxing and pleasurable and, in the case of the latter example, can prevent you from getting swept too far into an unknown rapid. Experienced canoeists are always willing to err on the side of caution and to maintain a preventative rather than a corrective mode of operation. This spares you the inconvenience and delays of recovering from a minor mishap or, in the case of a serious accident, the infinitely magnified problems of irreparable damage or loss of equipment or people.

The easiest lining situations occur in unobstructed but strong water. In ascending a shallow, steep pitch, you might find that the force of the current precludes poling the load or even an empty canoe. Tracking from shore or the shallows might just be the solution. It is hard going but easier than a full-fledged carry.

Perhaps you encounter a steep pitch in a downriver section of a trip. The rapid is open but shallow and full of steep waves. It is too shallow to paddle and too strong to pole. But with the weight of the canoeists removed from the canoe, the shortness and steepness of the waves are no longer so bad, and you could line the canoe down with complete confidence. Should conditions downstream improve or deteriorate, you could then paddle, pole, or portage the remainder as necessary.

Most other lining situations are related to more complicated and marginal conditions. Here there is no question regarding the possibilities of paddle and

Easy ascent along ledge. Ferry angle is wide in somewhat mild current to hold canoe just outboard of ledge rock. Note upstream-light, downstream-heavy trim.

pole. The risks are higher and the balances more delicate. Do we carry? Or can we line?

Achieving an answer begins by asking more questions. The first are the same considered for any type of in-river descent. What are the chances of broaching, of pinning a canoe in midstream, and of recovery should that happen? What is the river like below? Worse, better, pooled up, or is there a 100-foot falls around the first blind corner? What is the shoreline like? Is a portage difficult or easy, and at what point does it become impossible if we go too far? And finally, is there a feasible safe route to be lined, given the group's lining abilities?

Inevitably the well-made decision is a balanced judgment of conditions in relation to, and because of, the experience level of the party.

Before undertaking any serious lining problems on a trip, you should become familiar with the process in a programmed succession tending toward the more difficult as you accrue experience and finesse. First you should select a stretch of river that is shallow, unobstructed, and with just enough power to make a properly trimmed canoe ferry responsively. An unobstructed shore or shallows should be part of the selection too. Difficult footing, alder tangles, boulders, and cranky currents will come soon enough.

Before you place a light, waterproof load for proper trim in the canoe, wade out with the canoe all rigged for lining and swamp it. Even in a gentle introductory current, managing the canoe will be quite an experience. Remember that as the power and volume of the river increase, so will the forces on the lines. Rather than feeling like you have one runaway musk-ox on the end of a leash, you may feel like you have an entire herd pulling. In this way you will reduce complete, utter shock to eye-widening surprise for that coming occasion when the swamping is unintentional. You will also learn when to let go.

Now it is time to place a small load in the canoe, which will weight the downstream end to a point where the upstream end is tangent to or slightly out of the water. This is the same trim a poler would use and is the same regardless of an upstream or downstream direction of travel. The simple act of trimming is the difference between what is possible and pleasurable and what is troublesome and a curse. With the downstream end of the canoe deep, the current will always work for the liners by weather-vaning the canoe in the current. People are never stronger than gravity and large volumes of water, but at times they are smart enough to let these forces do some of the work for them.

The first basic rule for mild-current lining is that the upstream end of the canoe is nearly always toward midstream and the downstream end is snugged in closer to the shore from which the liners are working. This angle of set of the canoe in the current ensures that tension will be maintained on the lines as the canoe constantly tries to ferry away from shore. Yielding slack will move the canoe farther from shore, and retrieving line will move it toward shore. If the angle of set is maintained, the sidewash of the current passing under the canoe will keep the lines snug. Experiment with wide and narrow angles and observe the results.

Experiment with going up- and downstream and pay attention to the communication requirements of working with a partner. Each of you should switch positions from time to time and become fluent with both ends of the canoe and the techniques and differences related to each position. Many lining situations will require leapfrogging each other along a shore, and as with paddling, complete fluency in either position makes a better team.

Try solo lining also. In this case one person has both the bow and stern lines and is in a position to learn very clearly the difficulties of lining and to plunge to new depths of frustration, which are exacerbated by not having anyone at whom to direct misplaced blame. The solo traveler has no other option, but most of us will welcome tandem lining whenever possible. Still, solo lining is a great exercise and a skill well worth developing.

It is best to start with upstream work once you are familiar with the basics of set and the effects of current on a hull. Progress is slower in upstream travel, and observing the variables of cause and effect is easier and more readily sensible.

Ferrying occurs because the surge of water against the upstream side of an angled canoe tends to push the canoe away from the surge. If the canoe is held in place by snug lines that maintain the set, and if the liners are simultaneously moving upstream along the shore, the canoe should follow while maintaining its position a few feet off shore. If continued progress means passing to the outside of some rocks, the liners yield slack to the canoe, which then ferries further toward midstream because of the sidewash on an appropriate set. By balancing the set with the current to a point where the canoe will be held off the rocks on the outside while being pulled upstream, a scratchless passage is possible.

With no further obstructions to be passed, or if those that are there can be passed on the inside, then the liners draw the canoe in as close to shore as practical.

It is best to keep the canoe as close to shore as possible and, if the water and air are warm enough, to wade it up or down with a hand on the rail. Wading maintains the canoe in close and complete contact, and your footing improves if you can support yourself on the canoe. When it comes to letting the canoe out on the lines, work from as short a tether as possible. Control falls off dramatically the further away from you the canoe gets. Ideally the canoe will be only a few feet from shore; but all too often there will be times when it will be out toward the threshold of control, and a good many obstacles will lie between it and you. This latter condition is where confidence and expertise will be appreciated.

In upstream lining both liners are upstream of the canoe. With the bow person usually quite far forward and the stern generally just ahead or abreast of the canoe, both share in pulling the load upstream.

Generally, a high angle (tending toward broadside) to the current will move the canoe toward midstream with the most force. A low angle will ease your progress up- or downstream with little lateral pressure on the canoe. The liners must hold the tension on each line in a way that balances the set with steering requirements and the need to move forward. The amount of tension required will fluctuate constantly because of the nature of the riverbed and the resulting currents. The more complicated and rockstrewn the river, the more complex and intricate the process of lining becomes. Eddies, countercurrents, waves, drops, and holes will all conspire to help or hinder you in a bewildering array of forms and combinations.

In upstream travel, gravity and the force of falling water indicate instantly when lining is no longer possible and portaging is the way to go. If it is just too hard to move against the current, or if in attempting to pass a ledge the bow person has to release their line to let the canoe eddy out when the stern line catches it, then it's time to unpack and walk. Don't push it; the next hints the river delivers may not be so subtle or forgiving. A second attempt at that ledge may see your stern person desperately trying to slow a swamped canoe and work it into that eddy or, worse yet, having to release the stern line to avoid being pulled into the river. That would leave both of you safe on ledge but in the unenviable position of watching your canoe and gear lose hard-earned ground while you pray that it does not wrap and pin during its descent.

In descending a river, many elements of lining become reversed. The one constant is that the downstream end is trimmed heavy. In mild water the set is again with the upstream end toward midstream and thus held offshore by the sidewash. The same power of ferrying moves the canoe laterally, but in this case the current is providing power and carrying the load rather than opposing it. Because of this, travel is faster and, in moderate water, easier.

Ascending fairly strong water, but with an easily discerned route without complicated currents. Gear is packed to insure downstream heavy trim.

With bow-line tight and stern-line slack, liners let the current ferry a canoe outboard to the best channel, in preparation for descending a pitch.

Strong water in complicated rapids is another story. Going slow enough becomes a challenge, and the stern person soon spends as much time braking as maintaining the set. No longer is the upstream end outermost, as it may have been in milder water. Now it is snugged in close so the current will hold the canoe toward shore rather than threaten to rip the upstream end away, forcing the stern person to release the line. Only in carefully controlled moves is the stern let out to ferry wide and, once past the obstruction, it is quickly snugged in close. The liners must be constantly aware that in going downstream it is very easy to get sucked in too deep, only to find themselves in stronger water than they should be in. With the current carrying the load for you, it is easy to forget the levels of power you are dealing with until something gets a little out of hand and the control you once had vanishes without a trace. It is far better to predict this point in a descent than to let the river point it out to you.

During practice sessions in moderate conditions, using tension and slack in the lines to create proper angles is much like flying a kite. It is exciting as the canoe responds to the application of pressure set up by the lines and the force of the current. What is observed and learned at this level is the basis for successful lining and includes all the major elements. It is also where most of the literature on the topic and illustrations (if they get this far) leave off and thrust you out on your own to learn the hard way. This is the time to learn what angles are best in varying strengths of current and what can and cannot be done with the lines. Armed with knowledge gained on an open section of mild water, you are ready to encounter progressively more difficult situations—situations similar to those you will encounter on a trip where the way is full of boulders and eddies, drops, corners, ledges, holes, and standing waves. This is the part most books conveniently leave out, the part where lining takes on form and substance, where the kite flying suddenly has higher stakes, such as the value of your food and outfit.

The inconsistencies of fast broken water demand a much more analytical mind. Current lines will be the key to navigation now, and you must learn to know when the eddies and slack water can be used to advantage and when they will hinder you. Although some of the complexities can be helpful, others are not, and this is where your knowledge must be closely honed.

Following are some examples of typical situations and how best to deal with them. Remember, however, that text and examples remain only that. Your best teachers will be experience and empirical understanding. Confidence and judgment are as important as technical skill in manipulating the lines, and with patience, discipline, and continued practice, you will gain such expertise.

Situation 1: Upstream

A swift, navigable stream enters a lake, and the maps show another pond about a mile upstream. The contour lines indicate that the quick water will last only about half that distance and that the rest is flat water that leads to a marshy outlet. Just the place for moose, and it even looks like there will be some high ground for camping across from the moose marsh. The stream is too strong to pole but is quite open with good channels between the rocks. There are a few tight spots, but even so none of the eddies behind the boulders are too strong and none are large; most are less than half the length of the canoe. In some spots the water will probably be shallow enough to wade the canoe up.

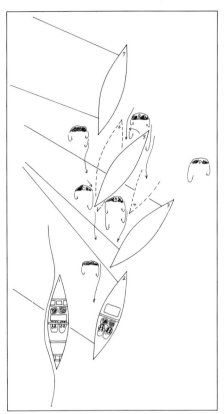

Situation 1

Having come from a few hours of lake paddling, the canoe has been trimmed flat, and to counter the difference in distance between the bow and stern seats and each end of the canoe, the load has been packed weight forward. The two food pack-baskets (the heaviest items) are right behind the bow quarter-thwart. The wanigan is just in front of the center thwart, and two people's gear is in waterproof gear bags behind the center thwart (canoe 1).

The first order of business after securing the lines is to retrim the canoe to lift the bow (upstream) stem an inch or two out of the water (canoe 2). The gear bags are moved aft far enough so that both packbaskets can fit behind the center thwart. The wanigan stays where it is, and the day packs and waterproof camera case are put in the space vacated by the stern paddler. The left shore looks the best, and it even looks like you can wade all the way up to the first boulders.

The scattered rocks are in water too deep to wade, and beyond the first few rocks is rock A, which will have to be passed on the outside. While moving upstream, increase the angle of set (canoes 2 and 3) so that the sidewash will move the canoe toward midstream, avoiding the eddy below rock A and positioning the canoe far enough outside so that the stern will clear rock A as it moves past it and into the eddy below rock B. Beyond the eddy line, the downstream current passes by harmlessly while the eddy itself holds the canoe in place, allowing a rest (canoes 4 and 5).

In that moment of rest you both decide that by backing the stern down between rocks A and C you can pass to the inside of rock B (canoes 5 and 6), which will keep the canoe out of the strong midstream water as well as keep it closer to shore. A gentle pull on the bow line gets the canoe out of the eddy and into a position to adjust the set and continue past rock B until the next rocks require additional maneuvering (canoe 7).

Situation 2: Downstream

After a fine evening of watching moose and exploring the pond, you decide that the following morning you will descend the stream to return to the main route.

In going downstream there are a number of instantly apparent differences. With the canoe facing downhill on a slightly inclined plane, gravity is helping rather than hindering forward movement. The effect of gravity on the water is revealed by the current, and the current is now carrying the canoe. When the force of the current had to be overcome on the upstream journey, the best route was close to shore where the water had less power and where rocks provided eddies to rest in. Now, with the current helping, you select a route to take the most advantage of deep water, which is also the strongest water, because of reduced friction from the bottom and sides of the riverbed.

Soon after leaving the marshy outlet, the river gets narrow and the current picks up speed. It is deep enough to paddle, but the bottom is clearly visible a little more than 3 feet below. Where the gradient steepens, the river becomes shallower and, in the main channel, swifter. It is a simple matter to pole down the stream keeping just to the edge of the main rush of water. This position is a little slower and, for the most part, requires only lateral corrections to keep the canoe in the best alignment which, with the exception of the tightest corners, is pretty much parallel to the flow. It takes no time at all to reach the point where you started lining upstream the day before at the first rocky section of quick water above the main lake.

At the crest of the rocky section you stop on the pole in a convenient eddy and look down the pitch. The stream narrows here to half its former width, providing a deep and strong channel. It is easily runnable on a paddle, then widens out over some gravel bars that would require a few hundred yards of poling to the lake below. You decide that the pitch is a great spot to practice downstream lining, knowing that later in the trip you will be doing some lining in earnest.

Earlier in the morning you had trimmed the canoe for normal paddling. It wasn't windy, and you packed for flat trim. At the start of the shallow quick water, you achieved poling trim by having the bow paddler kneel ahead of the bow seat and the stern person stand well ahead of the stern seat, actually bracing his forward shin against the rear quarter-thwart. Now, with no one in the canoe, it rests bow-heavy even without moving anything. To increase the bow weight, you place day packs and a camera case ahead of the bow seat, which lifts the stern (upstream) stem just a bit out of the water (canoe 1).

With the current carrying the load rather than opposing it, there is no need to make use of the eddies

behind the rocks, which are such useful resting spots when ascending. In fact the stronger water just outside rock B will yield a channel that requires little or no lateral movement once the canoe is lined up. The main concern is rock D, on the far side of rock B which, though easy to avoid, is positioned perfectly for a broach in the event of a miscalculation.

The first requirement is to establish enough set to get the canoe outboard of rock B. Once the stern is out far enough, the bow should yield some slack through controlled slip until the current swings the bow (canoes 2 and 3) into alignment for further descent. Because of the position of rock D, this should be done without delay. The angle of set should be decreased quickly to keep the current from pushing the canoe up on rock D. Once the canoe is realigned for descent, the current will quickly move it downstream, and if a slight set has been maintained as you each move along the shore, the canoe will avoid the eddies behind rocks B and A (canoes 4 and 5).

In downstream work there will be times when you can hold the canoe parallel to the current and let the current carry it. As a general rule, however, it is best to maintain a little set. This keeps tension on your lines and keeps you aware of the canoe's position even when you are not looking at it, such as when you are selecting footing for the next few paces or are glancing ahead to keep an eye on the overall route. In addition to maintaining tight lines, a little set means that the canoe is already engaged with sidewash and that there will be no lag time between establishing set and when the current takes effect.

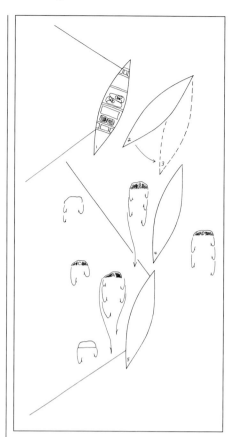

Situation 2

In ascending a stream, speed is considered only in terms of the speed of the current you are trying to overcome. It is slow going, and with the proper set there is always tension on the lines. You remain acutely aware that you are dragging a load uphill on a surface that is sliding in the opposite direction like a conveyor belt. Speed is also a factor in descent. Because the canoe is moving faster, you spend much of your time scampering along the shore to keep abreast of the canoe or applying the brakes and using eddies and slack water to slow the descent. You must be constantly aware of the canoe and your footing and ever vigilant in keeping tension on the lines.

The stern person will have an easier time maintaining tension. Half of their job is acting as a brake person, and this is pretty easy since their position onshore or in the shallows is nearly always upstream of the canoe. All lateral movements will require slowing or stopping the canoe for the sidewash to be effective. The person on the bow line will generally be downstream of the canoe. They will be controlling the set for the most part, but they must also be ahead of the canoe to pull it out of eddies or across current lines that are not going in the direction you want the canoe to go. When you are ahead of the canoe with the current coming toward you from behind, it is easy for the canoe to sneak up and introduce slack to your lines.

A little slack now and then won't amount to much. But in a tight spot, the canoe can lose its set and even adopt a set that is completely counter to your intentions. Too big a loop of slack could be swept around rocks in the water or tangled in brush, which might introduce tension when you don't want it from a direction you don't want. It is always easier to be frantically watching your footing and canoe, tightening your slack, and talking with your partner than to be frantically trying to untangle a situation that requires corrective measures.

It is nice to have things go as planned. Lining, or any other aspect of canoeing, seems easy then. You begin to believe you are getting pretty good. Fortunately, whenever anyone allows that thought to cross their mind, the river seems to know about it and concocts a little event to reintroduce some humility and caution. I much prefer to make a lot of little mistakes than to save up for a big one. Mistakes teach me far more than a program of always doing things correctly does, and smaller, comprehensible mistakes yield much to be analyzed. If you save up for a major disaster, you might just lose your gear in a manner so complex and complete that you can't really learn too much from it. Push your limits a little bit a lot of the time, and resist the temptation to take a flying leap at a higher level of accomplishment.

Let's return to the same easy pitch we just came through. This time, though, the river will introduce a little turn of events that will require a response that is performed quickly and well.

Situation 3A: Downstream—Recovering from an Unintended Spin

After setting up perfectly to drop down between rocks B and D by ferrying out toward midstream (canoe 1), the plan of progress unravels in a matter of seconds. It may be that the bow liner kept the bow in too close to rock B in combination with the stern liner being a hair overzealous in ferrying out toward stronger water. Of course none of these details matter at the moment; they can be analyzed after the event when a respectful, blamefree discussion might reveal the ingredients.

What matters in no uncertain terms is that the bow (canoe 2) is caught in the eddy below the rock and is being pushed upstream while, outboard of this, the strong current in the main channel is pivoting the canoe broadside above rock D. The bow person, who happens to be alert to this situation, moves immediately back upstream while pulling the canoe toward shore so that the latter half of the 18-foot canoe misses rock D. Simultaneously, the stern person lets go of the line to avoid being pulled into the river by the increased water pressure on the broadside canoe. "Line gone!" the stern person shouts, watching helplessly as the stern just clears rock D. The bow person hears and sees this and is able to move the bow a little upstream as the canoe finishes its 180-degree swing (canoes 3 and 4). Despite the slight upstream gain that yielded more swing space, the canoe thunks a bit on rock A (canoes 5 and 6) and pivots off to settle in the eddy below (canoe 7). "Nice save," the stern person says, "Sorry I lost the tail on you."

Once the stern person recovers their line, the canoe can be let down to a position where there is a clear spot wider than the canoe is long and twice its length. Here the bow person will step over the stern line and, when the stern person acknowledges readiness, give the bow a shove into the current, where the force of the water will spin it 180 degrees back into the proper orientation for continuing downstream.

When a recovery situation is performed well, we are all tempted to take full credit for success. In truth we can only claim a percentage; the rest belongs to luck. When

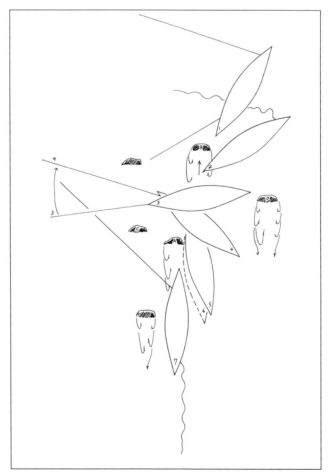

Situation 3A

something is done well, you never know how close you may have been to that fleeting and obscure interface between control and varying degrees of loss of control. At times we cross that line, recognize it, and jump back to the safe side. Other times the leap is too long and we feel that adrenergic surge of impending helplessness. At that point you simply do the best you can; stabilization will come in its own

time. For canoeists, this often means that something gets wet.

The most amazing and memorable element after a mishap is almost always how fast and suddenly everything seemed to happen. A fraction of a second of inattention here or there, a misapplied stroke, or a lapse in communication is all it takes to reveal that indistinct edge where control slips away.

Situations 3B & 3C: Downstream—Failing to Recover

We did well in that last recovery, but there were two other possibilities that we narrowly avoided by slipping precisely between them.

Our successful recovery involved an alert bow person who saw the potential situation and responded, even as the forces of the current

were conspiring to alter the plan. If instead the bow person had been looking down for better footing at the exact instant the bow got caught in the eddy and the stern line had to be released (canoe 8), and if a few feet of slack had caused a sag in the line, things might have been more traumatic. Had the canoe encountered rock D broadside and near the center of the hull, the force of the current would have been equal on both sides of the rock. With slack in the bow line and the stern line already free, there would have been nothing affecting the canoe but the current. The rock would have stopped the canoe, and the skin-drag of strong water passing under it would have quickly rolled the upstream gunnel under, instantly filling the canoe. It would have taken a few seconds or even minutes for the canoe to buckle and fold around the rock, and the sounds of the hull giving up would have been impressive indeed (canoe 9). Gear would have spilled or stayed with the canoe, depending on whether or not it had been tied in.

If after glancing at the ground for footing, the bow person had looked up just in time to ascertain that the bow had become caught in the eddy, the stern line was no longer

Situations 3B and 3C

functional, and a wrap on rock D was imminent, there would have been precious little time to react with corrective measures. A quick retrieval of slack and a pull of the line would have slid the canoe forward and almost clear of rock D (canoe 11). But just as a second pull was initiated, the stern would have caught and the bow would have swung down into rock A, bridging the two rocks (canoe 12). Again, the skin-drag would have rolled the upstream rail below the surface, and tons of water would have surged into and ultimately through the pinned canoe. The first comment in this scenario is likely to be, "Gee, too bad that rock wasn't a little farther away from the first." Or, "Too bad we didn't have a shorter canoe."

In all three of these examples there has been no negligence or single major factor leading either to an unscathed passage or disaster. It's really been nothing more than some elements of timing combined with good or bad luck. The fact remains that you must look for footing, that slack in the lines does occur, and that in the course of a day there are moments of inattention. The best that you can do is select the best possible timing for the ingredients of each process. Since the problem spots should be known and recognized when reading the rapid, it is easy to plan solid footing at those spots to yield undivided attention to the canoe and lines. Once the canoe is past potential danger spots and in calmer water, you can pick a route and skip along to the next spot that will yield the most control.

No one will ever recognize and cover all the possibilities, but that is what you should strive for, a closeness to perfection. Then things

will go right more frequently. Still, you must always be ready for those unexpected moments when a gust of wind or unobserved current calls for a quick response.

As your skills improve, lining will become like a dance. Each move is cooperative and carried out with precision. As the waters become stronger and more boulder-filled, you find that only one of you moves at a time, while the other maintains control until you are set up at the next station. Some conditions will require leapfrogging each other along the riverbank, alternating the bow and stern lines as you pass each other. There may be times in very difficult situations when the usual practice of each canoe team lining its own canoe will not be possible. Then a whole party might line up along a shore at various stations, and everyone will be part of a team that sees all the canoes through a pitch.

The basics that you learn in mild water will carry over to stronger and stronger water and to situations that become more complex. If you learn slowly and well, you will know pretty much what your capabilities are and when and how far to push them. The biggest difference you will encounter in strong water is that the topography of the river surface changes. Eddies become bigger and stronger, and there may be elevation changes along the eddy lines. Downstream rushing water may be inches or feet higher than the eddy water. Waves will be associated with holes, and the river will have a crown to it where the strong midchannel water is higher than the slower edge water.

The remaining examples will introduce a few more points of strategy. But by the time you encounter similar situations in the field, you will have learned as much.

Situation 4: Ascending Stronger Water

An ascent of a strong-water stream has gone smoothly and, being close to your present limits of expertise, has been exciting as well. Problems have been anticipated, theories have been correct, and your application of technique has been gratifying indeed. But, as always, there is a low drop above a strong eddy, and it all occurs on the outside of a curve. Better pause in the tail of the eddy where the water is not so strong and look things over.

At the upstream edge of the ledge the water is rebounding from the rock and is directed off toward midstream in a strong diagonal rush. Although only about a foot

The actual conditions are far better teachers than examples in books.

higher than the surface of the eddy just below the ledge, the water is strong in both the diagonal surge and in the eddy below. Just upstream of the ledge, the rock curves in a gentle arc and provides open shore and good footing in direct line with the surge off the ledge. A lot of line will be out, but the situation offers the only key to avoiding a lift-over, which means unloading and reloading the canoe to pass an obstacle that is less than the length of the canoe.

Because the river drops about a foot, there will be tremendous pressure on the bow when it first encounters the surge at the ledge.

In ascending a low drop the bow initially slices deep before rising up and over. This stage of ascent is when risk is greatest and speed is important.
Next, ascent is through fairly strong water, but with an easily discerned route without complicated currents. Gear is packed to insure downstream heavy trim.

Only perfect alignment of the canoe will prevent the current from tearing the bow away. The water pressure must be equal on both sides of the bow for the instant when it knifes through the surge and before the hull fills out to float the canoe up and over rather than slicing through the water. Speed is very important to minimize the time when the bow is deep and slicing. Even though the drop is low, trimming to raise the bow further is neither desirable nor possible.

There are no rocks outboard of the ledge nor below in the swing space should the bow be lost and the canoe have to spin into the safety of the eddy. This leaves only the eddy as a potential problem since the canoe will have to be just outside of its effect to avoid pivoting in the opposing currents on each side of the eddy line. There is a slight crown to the surge, so even if everything is aligned and outside of the eddy line, the canoe will tend to slide into the eddy from gravity. Speed will be essential even before the drop is encountered, and a very slight angle of set will be required to favor staying outboard of the eddy. At the instant the bow encounters the surge, all set will be eliminated, as anything but an orientation parallel to the current lines of the surge will tear the bow away.

To initiate the ascent you will have to back downstream a bit out of the tail of the eddy in order to get the canoe outboard of the eddy line. The stern liner will have to pay the most attention to yielding enough slack while maintaining enough tension to allow the canoe to stay

away from the eddy (canoes 1 and 2). The stern liner must also be completely ready to haul in the instant the bow encounters any difficulty. The bow liner will start at the tip of the ledge, position B-1, to ensure that the setup is well in place and, once it is, will have to move quickly upstream to position B-2 while simultaneously hauling the canoe upstream (canoes 3 and 4). There will be a moment when almost all the line is out, but since this is a direct pull straight up the current lines, any stretch in the rope will not affect the process.

Success or failure will be dramatic and fast. This move is an all or nothing situation that requires speed in both decision making and movement on the part of the liners and a clear pool below the ledge to make acceptable the risk of attempting to climb the drop. In the case of success there will be an exciting moment when the bow first slices into the surge with the water cutting around the stem right up to the outwales. As the bow line is hauled in quickly, it is only a fraction of a second before the canoe climbs the 4 or 5 feet forward and presents the ever widening hull to the surge, which now floats the canoe and raises the bow into the air at the rakish angle of a launched missile. Another second and the canoe is up and over and pulling easily now that the angle of climbing is decreased. Success is sudden, surprisingly easy, and all out of proportion to the care and precision of the setup and initiation of the move.

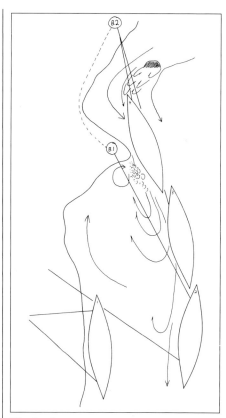

Situation 4

Situation 5: Recovering from a Spin

Failure unfolds equally fast and will happen if the canoe slides into the eddy during setup or if the bow is lost when the surge hits it. In the case of the eddy, you just back out and try again. In the case of a spin, you must get the bow facing back upstream before trying again. At worst the bow person might not let go soon enough in a spin, and this delay could swamp the canoe before it spins into the eddy with the stern liner's assistance. Or if the bow liner doesn't let go soon enough, they and the canoe might spin into the eddy, much to the merriment of the stern liner, who always gets a kick out of watching a fellow liner get snatched from solid footing to the water as if they were no heavier than a streamer fly on a light tippet (situation 5).

With an open pool and a strong eddy there is no danger to the canoe or load other than perhaps getting wet in a swamping. If you are packed well with good waterproofing systems, then there is nothing but a small delay in getting the water out of the canoe—a bargain when it comes to learning how powerful a surge you can overcome and what is best avoided. Knowing what not to attempt is as important a skill as everything else in your repertoire.

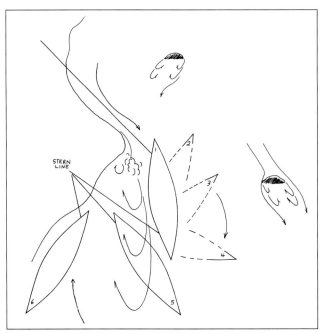

STERN LINE

Situation 5

Facing Page: Sequence showing loss of bow, stabilization by stern liner in eddy, re-alignment of canoe, and successful ascent on second attempt.

Situation 6: A Carry

When a similar diagonal surge is encountered without a curving upstream shore or accessible rocks that provide a pull-point directly in line with the surge, then there is no choice about attempting to line. You simply take the eddy right up to the ledge or rocks, unload, lift everything over, reload above, and continue upstream by the most appropriate means (situation 6). With a party of several canoes you may have enough people to get four on each side of a canoe and lift canoe and load across the ledge all at once. In Canadian Shield country, ledges of smoothness and good footing frequently allow this.

The same procedure would of course take place if there were rocks in the main surge or in the eddy that would prevent a 180-degree spin for recovery if the bow were lost.

During a hard day of travel where decision making is a constant requirement, it is actually a relief to encounter a place where your course of action is clear and simple. Although unloading and carrying may require physical effort and cause apparent delay, it is often a blessing in disguise, especially for the leaders.

No thinking, weighing, and evaluating. You just get out and do it. The mind rests. And nothing need be said about the delays that would compound themselves after recovering from a reckless attempt at something that never should have been tried in the first place.

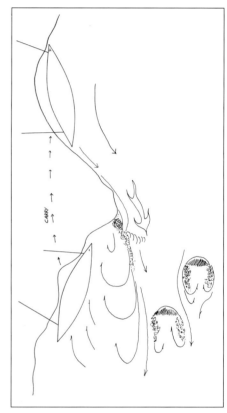

Situation 6

Situation 7: Downstream in Strong Water

When navigating the larger rivers of the North, there are often sections of continuous, awe inspiring rapids. As the trip progresses and leaves the higher ground of headwaters and smaller rivers, there are a number of huge, magnificent waterways that often run for hundreds of miles before reaching salt water in such places as Ungava Bay and the Chantrey and Chesterfield inlets. Rapids a half mile wide or more are not uncommon, and the power of these waterways is nothing short of stupendous. Even so, at the very edges of the rapids there are often sneak routes where the skilled liner can proceed with style and élan.

Depending on the nature of the ledges, eddies, pools, drops, or long, even downgrades, the skilled liner can negotiate some surprisingly rough water. As always, it is the diagonal currents to watch out for and any situations where very strong water can tear the upstream end of the canoe away from the stern liner. In the milder currents of smaller streams, the liner can work with the upstream end a little outboard of shore so that the ferrying action holds the canoe toward midstream; but in heavy water, the liner is almost always holding the stern in snug, which means the current keeps the canoe pressed against the shore. The only times this closeness is relaxed are in specific instances where calm spots in the rapid will safely allow for ferrying outboard to get around something. Generally the water is too strong for this, and the risk of the current peeling the upstream end away from shore and spinning the canoe is too great.

In rough-water lining, problems are generally related to the height of waves and whether or not they are breaking. The biggest danger in rough-water lining is swamping and then trying to hold several tons of water-filled canoe in a strong current. Using a spray cover with the cockpit openings cinched tight allows for some remarkable descents. With the cockpits nearly closed, very little water gets into the canoe unless it rolls and remains inverted for any length of time. Even if a canoe is rolled, it fills slowly enough to be stabilized before the weight becomes too much of a problem. With most rough-water lining being done very close to shore with a set that keeps the canoe pressed toward shore, potential accidents retain a reasonable degree of controllability; even if the stern liner must snub his line around a rock to hold the canoe, it will likely be right along the shore.

Any lining done in an area where a mistake can result in the canoe being peeled away from shore is a judgment error made in advance of the liners committing themselves to disaster.

The major point to remember is that in going downstream it is very easy for the current and the momentum of the canoe to lure you into stronger water than you should be in. Remember your limits and what to watch out for, and keep your lines tight. Pay attention to your level of doubt and fear. Elect to carry before you reach the threshold of uncertainty. In heavy water there may not be many warnings from the river until you find yourself on the wrong side of that threshold.

Situation 7 shows a canoe with spray cover being let down a strong chute snug along the edge. Even if the first wave breaks over the canoe and a little water gets through the bow cockpit (canoe 2), the canoe will slide off the edge of the waves into the eddy by gravity because the tongue of the surge through the chute will be considerably higher than the surface of the eddy. The liners can then pull the canoe across the eddy regardless of where the current wants the canoe to go and, if they wish, can snug it up to shore to check for water inside.

Oftentimes, even in a huge, high-volume rapid, there will be so many rocks along shore that the water at the edge of the river behaves much like a rapid in a smaller, gentler stream. Here you can line in relative safety. The eddies of course will help and hinder as usual, but the main power and force of the water are outside in the deeper channels,

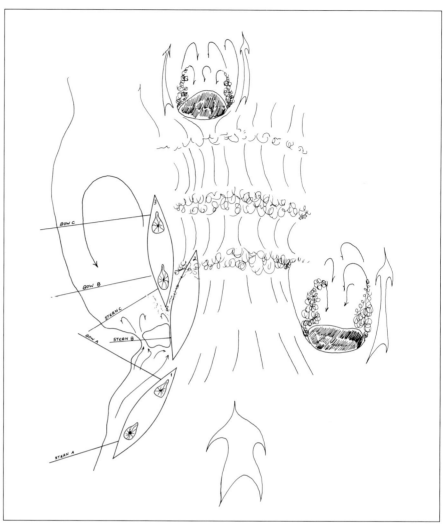

Situation 7

rushing by dramatically and harmlessly beyond the fringe of sheltering
boulders. Many times you can slip
through such a sneak route in Class
II water while, a few hundred yards
out, the main river is a frothing
train of crowned-up, canoe-gob-

bling waves breaking and exploding
a good 10 feet above the water level
at shore edge.

The best approach is always to be
smart first, careful second, and then
line skillfully if you choose to
proceed.

Fine Points

Coils and Tangles

In the process of becoming skilled at setting angles, hauling, braking, and flying
the canoe like a kite, you will discover that your vocabulary regarding the lines
disintegrates with alarming frequency to a few all-purpose expletives. It doesn't
take long for lines to become animate objects bent on frustrating whoever is
trying to keep them in orderly flat coils that can be let out or taken in without
so much as a glance. Occasionally lines behave, usually on nice flat outcrops of
granite that are so smooth not even glacial striations appear on their polished
surface. It seems that a misanthropic line knows it is not worth trying to get
hopelessly tangled on a surface too smooth to yield a lot of snags and points.

But just wait until you are lining in thick willows interspersed with blowdowns, boulders, and your own flailing feet, with the accompaniment of countless blackflies swirling around your head net. No line on the planet could resist fouling on every available discontinuity in a situation like that. It takes nerve and concentration even to remember that somewhere, wherever the other ends of those blanketyblank lines are, is a canoe with all your worldly possessions in it.

The most you can hope for is a saintly sense of patience and immunity from abject frustration. It also helps if you know a few tricks that limit a line's ability to scramble itself into inscrutable, spontaneous knots.

Canoe liners quickly become superb rope coilers. It is an activity that constantly occupies the hands and soon becomes unconscious. The best liners even become ambidextrous from working different sides of the rivers. A coil length of 15 inches seems to be about optimum for most situations. This means that a bit more than 30 inches of line are let out or retrieved with each loop. Because the loops making up the coil are relatively short, their tendency to relax into figure eights is reduced. With the coil hanging flat, loops are free to spill off when yielding slack in an even manner, with the amount of slip being controlled by the free hand, which should be the one closest to the canoe (left when on the right streambank, right when on the left streambank). If you are not an ambidextrous coiler, you can coil with your favored hand and then turn the looped coils as a unit 180 degrees so the loops will fall toward the canoe in a release. This will prevent twisting and knotting that would occur if the releasing of loops were to take place on the shore rather than canoeside of the coil. Being

In preparation for dropping through a pitch too shallow to run on a paddle and far too strong to pole, the stern liner stabilizes the canoe while bow moves ahead to position 1. With bow person ready, the stern liner wades out to best position and slowly lets canoe through the first drop (2) while the bow liner retrieves slack. With lines tight in both directions the canoe is let down at the edge of the rough water (3) in preparation for sliding into a narrow eddy (4) where it can rest until liners are positioned for the next series of moves. Gear has been moved forward to insure proper trim.

1

2

3

4

left-handed, I line better from the left shore. On the right shore I turn the coil around when I'm not disciplined enough to practice ambidexterity.

The other reasons for short coil lengths are related to reducing the tangling potential among bushes, rocks, and the liner's feet. Not only do such tangles usually require the liner to backtrack to free up tangled loops, but a snagged line can be disastrous if slack is urgently needed for the canoe itself, for the liner to move ahead to better control points along the shore, or if the next step requires tossing the remaining coil ahead to the other liner or liners.

Although at the time it always seems persnickety and time consuming to be constantly maintaining neat, short coils, it is invariably worth the effort. It is a habit that will yield the easiest passage achievable as well as keep your frustration level low enough to be manageable or ignorable.

Knots

Constantly keeping 40- or 50-foot lines coiled well sooner or later prompts the following question: Why in the name of Eddie Bauer and L. L. Bean don't we just use shorter blanketyblank lines in the first place and tie some blanketyblasted longer tails on if we need them? A good question, and in fact some canoeing texts actually recommend exactly that. But to do so requires a knot in the line, and if there is to be one hard and fast rule in the art of lining, it should be *no knots ever.*

The first thing a knot in the line will do is pass between two rocks and wedge itself. This is bad enough when it happens onshore where a person can walk over and back the knot out, but if it happens underwater and is inaccessible, then you and your canoe are in serious trouble. A knot that gets caught may well upset the canoe, and a canoe full of water will never yield enough slack to back out the knot, assuming you can even get to it. An accessible pocket knife is supremely appreciated in such a situation.

Even a line without a knot in it is more than capable of getting stuck between rocks or wrapped around them. Snagging is to be avoided whenever possible, and the no-knot rule is a good addition to the habit of always keeping free line neatly coiled.

It is of course remarkably tempting to add additional line *just this once* or in any variety of special situations where things will probably go well if extreme caution is exercised. And it might just work when the problem factors are acknowledged and recognized. Such reasoning has three caution flags in it for me, however; *probably, if,* and *might.* But then I'm not a gambler and seldom assume probability is in my favor.

The terminal ends of my lining ropes have always had end splices that yield a slight tapered thickening at the very ends. They let me know by feel where the ends are and so far none have become chocked between rocks. The braids of the end splices are quite compressible and have always pulled through any areas where a knot would have wedged and stuck. Despite this good record, I think the next generation of lines I make will terminate in a whipped end the same diameter as the rope itself. Since I prefer white or light-colored rope for visibility, I will whip on a section of black thread 6 feet before the end as a visual cue that rope is out. A simultaneous cue will of course be revealed by the lack of remaining loops in my coil-retaining hand.

Gear: Tied in or Free

Canoeists could spend their remaining evening campfire discussions reviewing the advantages and disadvantages of whether or not to tie gear into the canoe during travel. After all that discussion, I'm not sure anyone would be any closer to a simple answer or to any rules of procedure. I have observed three main camps regarding the topic: those that always tie in gear; those that never tie in gear; and those that sometimes do and sometimes don't, depending on a long list of qualifying factors. I have at various times been a member of each of these camps, though my most recent and longest allegiance has been to the sometimes camp. The first two camps have it easy—perfectly defendable positions based on sound arguments—and this is what gave rise to the sometimes camp. The hard part is knowing under what conditions to tie gear in.

The crux of the matter has to do with the supposed recoverability of canoe and gear in the event of a serious accident. The never-tie-in folks assume that in the event of a wrap and pin that is inaccessible, it would be great if most or all of the gear spilled from the canoe and eventually washed into an eddy where it could be recovered. Of course in a high-volume, brawling river, recovery might not occur; the stuff might simply get away and not be found. But at least the chances of getting some items back are improved.

The always-tie-in folks remain convinced that gear tied in acts as flotation, minimizes the probability of a wrap, and if it is secured in a canoe that wraps, will increase the chances of recovering that canoe—which of course assumes it is accessible. These folks would rather wrestle with a big contained unit and not get people all split up running after free parcels that are washing away down rapids and over falls to who knows where.

Both opinions are sound. Each has many good points regarding disaster management of both people and gear. Each has insolvable aspects in some situations, and none of the situations are entirely predictable. It is the quintessential "damned if you do, damned if you don't" scenario. A complete loss of outfit is possible in either case.

The sometimes folks are the chronic evaluators. If three parties—one of each type—arrives at the head of a rapids, the first two will read the rapids and be on their way. The sometimers will read the rapids, look at the topographic sheets to see what is coming up downstream, and then start looking at the type of rapid, the volume of water, and a zillion other factors, hoping that in the end more reasons will accumulate for one option than the other and that the issue will be settled.

In all three cases an unknown but potential risk is evaluated in terms of how best to recover should something happen. It may be that nothing happens, or if it does, it may not be what was predicted. The decision of tying in or not is therefore based on so much speculation that in the end everyone does pretty much what they prefer to do rather than adopt a scientific strategy. In a very serious mishap, gear recovery could be a moot point. In the end, despite your arsenal of reasons and applied thought, the whole thing is still a fifty-fifty proposition. What is different, however, is your level of confidence of approach based on your knowledge of options and potentialities. Whatever yields the most confidence is the best strategy, provided that an in-river attempt at passage rather than a portage is still within the realm of reason.

Spray Covers

If you travel with spray covers, the covers will hold everything in. Because covered canoes often repose upside down after a roll, however, some travelers go so far as to tie in covered gear, which stabilizes everything in the event of an upset. If loose gear balloons the cover to its maximum stretch while the canoe is upside down, the weight of the load settles at the lowest point and the hull is buoyed by trapped air. The result is a canoe that remains upside down with remarkable stability. Liners using crotched lines are at a great advantage in such a case. With the pull-point of the lines on the bottom of the hull, the canoe can often be rolled upright, which resettles the gear. If there is not too much water inside, the canoe may retain some manageability while you regain control.

Spray covers allow for some remarkable canoeing from both a paddling and lining point of view. If you choose to use them, a good guideline is to accept their benefits regarding rain and spray from waves and the increased potential for passage in heavy water but also to retain a sense of their limits. It is easy to get used to attempting very rough water, and a résumé of successful runs can easily lure you into water that should not be attempted in remote settings. That shifty and illusory line that marks the limits of control is probably nearer than you think.

In the context of lining, spray covers make possible some very tricky descents. But you must choose carefully where to push the limits. It is one thing to experiment in a pool and drop river and quite another to do the same on a huge river of high volume, power, and speed in combination with long sections of a steep gradient.

My friend George Luste of Toronto is a veteran of northern waterways. Once, on the headwaters of the Notakwanon in Labrador, he returned to his party after scouting ahead along continuous rapids. "Some unconventional lining is ahead," he said. Some of his party wondered what that might mean and soon found out. George cinched his cockpit covers closed, took up his lines, and proceeded to the first notch between boulders where the entire headwater stream funneled over a 4-foot drop. There was a deep pool below with sufficient distance to the next drop for George to have seen the possibilities. The canoe launched itself between the rocks at the crest, gathered the momentum of the current, and dropped to the pool below, the bow plunging almost to the quarter thwart before surging to the surface as its buoyancy overcame the momentum of the dive. Water streamed from the cover in an impressive manner and the drama of the event was nearly eclipsed by George's grin when success repeated itself as the party continued downstream. Traces of that grin return when he tells the story; he looks like a boy who has skillfully stolen some cookies and gotten away with it.

Wear and Tear

Lining causes the most wear and tear of all the elements of canoe usage while in the bush. It is surpassed only by the ravages of the rivets on float-plane pontoons and unpadded canoe racks on shuttle vans. Abrasion is not limited to the underwater part of the hull, though that area receives the most. With so much maneuvering in and around rocks and ledges, often with light contact or pivoting a deliberate part of the passage, everything from the rails down seems to absorb some wear. If the spray covers come down over the rails, as most do, the edges often suffer from sneaking along granite ledges. Many people sew on additional strips of cordura or canvas at the edge of the rail.

Canoes of different materials suffer in different ways, but none are immune to the rigors of lining. The ABS canoes with their great impact resistance are horrible when it comes to abrasion. Canoes with synthetic or aluminum rails often get sharp little slits and burrs along them. Kevlar and fiberglass canoes show the myriad scratches and light gouges in the form of a whitish fuzz which increases friction on the hull. The wood and canvas canoes we use tend to lose the shellac coating below the waterlines, and the wooden rails get a bit fuzzy from sliding along rocks and ledges. Whatever the materials of the craft you choose, be prepared for some visible wear.

Liners are quick to experience some wear and tear of their own. Bad footing along most rivers is self-explanatory. If you value your knees, shins, ankles, and arches, be careful. One item that is easily overlooked on a trip at least once (though seldom twice) is a big supply of hand cream. You may already have found a need for hand cream while paddling and poling, but if not, lining is sure to introduce you to chronically chapped hands. The constant handling of wet line in cold air that is always wet, dry, windy, or sunny can lead to cracks and fissures through which you feel like you should soon be able to see your finger bones. The pain of a bad case of cracked, abused hands is remarkable.

The time I forgot hand cream in Labrador has never allowed me again to forget a tube of concentrated cream such as Neutrogena. After six days of ascending an unnamed river, I could hardly pull on a sock without feeling sick with the pain in my cracked and bleeding fingers. Adhesive tape backed with vegetable oil provided a quick and effective cure, but the oil supply had a few more weeks to go and I knew that with my penchant for eating well, a reduction in the amount of oil available for medical purposes might have to be enforced in the interest of bread and pancakes and more. Fortunately it never came to that; I learned to carry hand cream and never had to choose between pie crust and comfort on that particular trip.

Stowing Lines

After you have mastered the geometry and physics of lining and have become a wizard at ambidextrous coiling and handling, the only point left is stowage of lines when not in use.

If part of your route has several hundred miles of lakes or easy going, it may be best to pack the lines away somewhere safe and secure in your dunnage. This will make it impossible for them to be lost on a carry, misplaced, or in the way in the canoe.

If you have use for them periodically and have not rigged a good system for secure stowage on the canoe, then this is a good option. Since I use crotched lines that are secured to the seat frames, I simply untie one tail and wind the line up by passing it around the small carrying thwart behind the decks and back to the seat frame until all slack is used. Only enough free line is left to tie off the end securely. It takes time to do this, but the line is secure, completely out of the way, and stored parallel to the rail. It can't come out by mistake during portaging or any other activity.

An equally effective storage method is to have two permanent light lines attached in the rib spacings (or you can drill special holes if you don't have slotted rails) to tie neatly coiled line to through the bundle of loops. This saves you the time of feeding the line around thwarts and seat frames. Releasing the light lines and reattaching the free tail to the seat frame after passing it under the canoe restores your readiness to line.

Many travelers rig a bit of shock cord across their decks and stow their coiled lines under it. This is fine for onwater temporary storage when use is frequent, but this is not an arrangement suitable for portaging. Sooner or later the line at the stern will catch on the ground or a branch and uncoil until it snags on something and snubs the canoe to a dead stop while the carrier has all the momentum of full stride. This is never pleasant and can cause injury beyond the usual loss of the carrier's temper. It is no fun to put a load down just to recoil an errant line, especially one that adds a pulled back or whiplashed neck to the inconvenience.

When the Peake brothers of Ontario and British Columbia were on a fifty-five-day trip to name the Morse River in honor of the late Eric Morse, they learned not to leave the lines attached during a portage. Despite the fact that the line was secured to the lining loop in the stern by a carabiner and was tucked under a tight shock cord on the stern deck, the line came free on a carry. The loss remained undetected for the remainder of the day. Two members of the party got to paddle eighteen miles back to the carry and then search for the line. The carry was on open tundra so there was no fixed route across it, which vastly increased the area to be searched. Two points are well revealed in this anecdote. One is the importance of lining lines on a long trip; the other is the importance of stowing the lines for the carries.

In the thick of a day that includes combined running on a paddle or pole, wading, and lining, it is often tempting just to throw the coils in the canoe between periods of use. This is done because it seems easier and quicker. Inevitably it sets you up for a longer delay later when you try to untangle the mess that results from the loose coils being kicked around to keep them out of the way. More importantly, loose lines can endanger you in the event of an accident. If the canoe swamps or capsizes while paddling a section of rapids, fifty feet of loose line swirling around you and the canoe is no joke. If you become entangled and the current is rushing a swamped canoe downstream, you are in serious danger of being dragged to your doom.

The small amount of time it takes to trouble yourself with proper stowage will always be worth it. Take the time. A life jacket should always be considered mandatory lining equipment. Chances are you will already be wearing it because of the nature of a river that might require some lining. But occasionally you may have to remind yourself to put it on. Although lining should be conducted with solid footing as part of the process, things can happen. You could be knocked over by strong current while wading, pulled by an errant canoe, or you might slip in off a ledge or rock. It is best to be prepared for the few times this may happen by wearing your life vest.

Keep an eye on the areas of high wear on the lines, usually the 8 or 10 feet closest to the canoe. The fibers here will abrade, and sharp rocks may even slice a few strands now and then. After especially hard sections or after a day of much lining, it pays to check.

After a few years' use it may be time to replace your lines. The synthetics break down in sunlight over time, and often the fibers suddenly seem to abrade with increased speed. The strands probably have grown brittle with age and exposure, and it is time to replace them.

With care, tracking lines should last a reasonably long time. May your relationship with them be marked by smooth, flat coils and a lack of tangles. If you are less lucky than this, then keep a ready sense of humor—as well as a lexicon of ingenious curses.

4

Crossing Land:
The Ways of the Portage Trail

We are on top of the Big Hill portage tonight...It rises 700 feet in a quarter mile...Up this on some tortured back has come every one of the thousands of traps above the Big Hill, every tin stove, every Dutch oven, every bag of flour that ever nourished a hunter in this far country. Beyond this point every article of God's manufacture, or man's, undergoes a change in status. The value of merchandise is not calculated here by the currency of any nation on earth, but by weight and utility. A pound of tea is worth more than a diamond ring and ten pounds of flour is worth more than twenty pounds of gold.
True North by Elliott Merrick -1933

During an extended traverse of the wilder waterways, the time will come when the heights of land between drainages will need to be crossed or the difficulty of rapids will exceed the potential of navigation by poling or lining. Portaging will be the means to continue travel beyond the reaches of the present watershed or to circumnavigate unrunnable canyons and rapids that punctuate the route.

For some, the anticipation of upcoming portages looms as a large and un-pleasant element of the trip and can even detract from the experience as a whole. It is likely that the portages will be the most physically and mentally demanding parts of a trip, particularly in untrailed country. Whether you antici-pate portaging with dread or with pleasure, the keys to maximum ease of pas-sage will be the same. Your savvy as a traveler will be revealed by the carries of canoe country because it is here that your organizational, route-finding, and group-management skills and load division and delegation will highlight finesse or disorganization.

I suppose I should admit at the outset that I like portaging. By this I don't mean that I can find some perverse joy in hard, awful going or when the view and quality of the air perceived from the inside of a bug net on a humid day leaves much to be desired. I like portaging when the loads are slipped back to the ground, when the despair and cursing are over. Such depths only heighten the sense of accomplishment and achievement. Rather than look at the carries as daunting and difficult obstacles, look at them as gateways to distant interiors, gates that stop the less possessed or the less skilled, gates that preserve the wilder-ness for those who go beyond. There is a smugness to be reveled in when navi-gation has been precise and a large amount of gear has been efficiently handled and delivered with a minimum of frustration and pain. No other aspect of ca-noe travel, short of living from the land, yields such a clear vision of autono-mous freedom and independence.

There is nothing quite like the feeling you get when traveling into new terrain knowing that behind you are a string of rapids that have been ascended or circumnavigated and a string of tiny lakes full of sky that yielded a route to high ground, ground that will fall away soon and yield another chain of lakes and rivers to be followed. These are the jewels on a necklace of accomplishment, a hallowed ground known mostly to the indigenous people and the few who like yourself have learned the secret rewards of going beyond those gateways that winnow the less curious and less ambitious. A good many of those gates will come in the form of portages, and anyone can portage.

Of course the other realities of portaging exist. There is always deep mud or steep bouldery areas with poor footing, blowdowns, heat, bugs, compass bearings that contain errors, fatigue, discouragement, and all sorts of things that are likely to prompt profanity. The trick is to minimize these elements, to become skilled at acceptance when avoidance fails, and to learn to adjust loads for the vagaries of terrain, finding the combinations that yield safety, passage, and possibility.

Most of us learn our basic canoeing in somewhat of a package form from camps or outdoor education centers or from people who got their basics from such a place. It seems that something in human nature makes us recall and adopt those packages with great fidelity and often as "the way" things should be done. Part of this may be age related; we were all very impressionable during the years we were most likely to be exposed to a canoe camp. Whatever the origins may be of what in adulthood becomes a narrow provincial view, we can benefit greatly from viewing the wider horizons provided by all the different canoeing traditions. In this way we can select and mix those elements that most closely match our needs.

The methods of portaging, as reflected in different areas of canoe country, reveal a great deal about the similarities and differences between these areas. For the most part, the canoeing traditions that have evolved show specific adaptations that correlate to the landscape of origin. The wide-ranging voyageur can thus benefit greatly by assessing all of these strategies.

Rather than rehash the specifics of these various methods, some of which are described in detail in other texts, this chapter looks at how to think about, evaluate, and adapt various strategies to a wider range of wilderness trails and the personalities of those who will traverse them.

When canoeists meet at an event that draws paddlers from the full breadth of northern canoe country, it is readily apparent in what geographic area the traveling paddlers cut their teeth. The Canadians come with their favorite Woods packs and, if they are from southern and mid-Ontario, a number of wanigans and waterproof duffle bags along with neatly coiled or attached tumplines. The Minnesota gang will be on hand with their fairly short canoes, which all seem to have fixed portage pads on a special carrying thwart, and they themselves will be dwarfed by their size 3 or 4 genuine Duluth or Duluth-style packs. Mainers will stand out because of their long canoes, setting poles, pack baskets, and penchant for standing up in canoes. New Yorkers from the Adirondack country will recognize the pack baskets, and the Vermonters, who are located near everybody else, are likely to have a little of everything.

Although this crew of canoeists may be polite and appear accommodating of their differences, deep down there will be a few points of opinion that are not negotiable. Much as we might learn from each other, there is a part of each of us that knows that what we subscribe to is the "right" way. It is as simple as that since the premise is purely subjective. And it is correct even beyond that subjective pose. It is correct because all the techniques and methods are refined functional strategies for canoe travel in specific areas. Each method will function very well wherever it is traditionally applied in the northern reaches of canoe country, and better still, a hybridized methodology derived from the best of all traditions will custom tailor a means of graceful canoeing and portaging to each individual.

Canoe equipment must accommodate both water and land travel. It must be ready to survive not only extended rains but potential dunking and even prolonged immersion. Packs must fit both the canoe and the portager's back with equal ease. Materials must be abrasion resistant, not prone to solar breakdown, and not much influenced by radical swings in temperature. Methods of carrying should be efficient, while using the musculature and skeletal systems of the human frame to best advantage.

In addition to these factors are those that make life in camp easier. Do the packs lend themselves to easy organization and access? Can they be waterproofed for the protection of food and personal gear? Mistakenly rehydrated dried food and soaked sleeping bags are inconveniences best avoided in the first place.

The landscape itself will have a significant role in determining the methods of packing and travel, and finally, the nature, stature, and level of fitness of the individuals on a trip will have a bearing on what types of equipment are selected.

Duluth-style Packs

The Duluth-style packs have their origin in the American Midwest, where one of the first manufacturers was the Duluth Tent and Awning Company of Duluth, Minnesota. The packs were good enough and serviceable enough that the generic name was applied to all such packs. Originally made of canvas, these packs are now made by dozens of manufacturers in both canvas and synthetic pack-cloth fabric. The best are fitted with high quality straps, roller buckles, and tumplines and are built to last. The beauty of the Duluth pack is that it is simple in shape and concept and smart in the placement of straps, buckles, and doubled cloth or leather patches on the bottoms and abrasion points. These are packs that thrive in the granite country of the Boundary Waters and Quetico regions.

Equipment

Duluth style pack with combined shoulder straps and tumpline, with a waterproof tent bag stacked on top.

Just north of this area, the Canadian counterpart is found in the Woods packs, which are similar in simplicity, function, and ruggedness, though of a slightly different design. The Woods company is no stranger to the needs of those who require packs that can stand the rigors of hard, sustained use. The forest-fire crews of Canada's Ministry of Natural Resources have relied on the Woods packs for fire-hose packs for generations, as have the canoeists who have adopted them.

The original Duluth packs evolved in a land of countless and often steep, relatively short portages. The ratio of land to water encountered on a Minnesota canoe trip has prompted some sly observations. A famous Maine canoe builder who brought his building and travel skills to the Boundary Waters area had a variation on the state motto of "Land of 10,000 Lakes;" to it he added the clause "None of them connected by navigable water."

This comment reveals the most important reason behind the traditional preference for short, light canoes and single, huge packs by those who ply the Boundary Waters. In a land where a half-day paddle may see five or ten portages, canoeists have precious little interest in keeping track of many small packs. Efficiency is realized by packing everything in a few large-volume packs with nothing scattered randomly in the canoe. Generally, these carries are short enough to inspire a tendency to shoulder fairly heroic loads. A size 4 pack with the bulky but lighter clothing and shelter outfit in it can be stacked atop a denser and heavier pack that contains the food. Whoever is carrying the canoe may simultaneously carry a smaller pack, if one is along. The beauty of the Duluth style is that many sizes are available, allowing travelers to mix and match loads to accommodate a variety of people from the smallest children to the largest adults. The minimum total number of packs makes for a minimum of fuss when unloading and loading at each end of a carry.

Since these packs are essentially large, open sacks with a good cover, it is up to the individual to compartmentalize the interiors for organizational purposes and waterproofing. Items grouped in lined stuff-sacks make for easy organization and provide the option of double waterproofing gear or increasing water resistance if the whole pack is also lined. Anything that diversifies options and allows a range of adaptations is generally good. One way of lightening the load is to maximize the use of multifunctional gear, and this style pack is great for that.

On a very long trip, when a food pack becomes empty or when its contents can be consolidated into another pack, it can be rolled or folded up and put in the bottom of a pack that is still being used. Or, when day packs or camera cases are along on the trip, these smaller items can be consolidated into the now empty big pack to make the carries more efficient and enjoyable.

Wanigans

Wanigans are wooden boxes designed to fit in a canoe and be carried by tumpline over the portages. Although a few companies are attempting to manufacture synthetic wanigans, often making them waterproof, most of these attempts are not very satisfactory in the eyes of serious travelers. For the most part, those who use wanigans still make their own from pine boards or light plywood. These wanigans range from the elaborate and carefully compartmentalized models that would make a cabinet maker proud, to a simple box with a lid. I prefer the simple-box approach because it has the most versatility and represents the least amount of loss if bears make kindling of it or a rapid pounds it up a bit.

Wanigans make great low tables in the kitchen for kneading bread dough and rolling out pie crusts and for keeping food and utensils out of the sand or muck or moss. Some are made strong enough to sit on, but this is often discouraged by those who want them light or wish to preserve the surfaces for kitchen functions.

On the carries, a rigid box yields a stable platform for stacking additional loads. Since it is carried by means of a tumpline and therefore with extreme efficiency, the additional weight can be handled easily.

The epicenter of wanigan use is in the Temagami region of Ontario where several of the more renowned canoeing centers have a long and busy history. Here the use of the tumpline is not mysterious, and it is the tumpline that makes the use of wanigans possible and desirable. Elsewhere in canoe country, the use of the tumpline is regarded as a curiosity that is not much understood, and their use is fading. In the United States, tumplines survive on some of the Duluth packs as standard accessories and among canoeists who make their own after having been introduced to them in Canada, Maine, or, in many cases, the histories and material culture texts of the North.

For those fluent with the use of the tumpline, the wanigan is a useful tool and a great asset to have in a traveling kit.

Pack Baskets

New York's Adirondack region, Maine, New Brunswick and, to a lesser degree, the St. Lawrence River are the areas where Black Ash pack baskets are part of the canoe culture. Black Ash, which grows in the flood-silt areas and swamps along certain waterways, has the unique property of splitting out along the growth rings when pounded repeatedly. The Micmacs, the Penobscots, and the Passamaquoddies remain to this day the finest craftspeople for both fancy baskets and pack baskets. Unfortunately, not enough pack baskets are made to supply the market, and good pounded ash baskets are essentially unavailable to all but those who have access to a form and can make their own.

Stacked load on wanigan carried by tumpline. Wanigan, waterproof camera case, daypack and tripod complete the load.

Nevertheless, pack baskets are a fine item for canoe travelers. They are light, rigid, and when made from pounded ash, incredibly strong and resilient. The splints that make up a pounded ash basket contain only the tight grain of the summer-wood section of a growth ring within the tree. The porous spring-wood section of the ring is the line of separation between each strip and is what caves in from the pounding. A good pounder can peel up to seven or ten growth rings from each pounding along the length of a log, and from these are shaped and beveled the splints that make up the weavers and standards of a basket.

Ash baskets that are available commercially are generally made from sawn White Ash with palm rattan weavers. They are weak, prone to splitting, and don't last long enough under hard usage to be worth considering when compared to pounded ash baskets.

Canoeists who somehow acquire or make their own pack baskets, however, will discover a versatile pack that is wonderfully adapted to the canoe and carry. Because they are rigid, they are self-standing around the campsite kitchen which keeps them clean, easy to organize, and easier to root through when looking for ingredients. Not only does the rigidity protect the contents from external forces, but it also protects the backs of portagers from any odd-shaped or hard-edged items that are packed within. When lined with a rubberized liner for waterproofing, even very dense and heavy food packs will float, and the resilient weave will afford protection against dropping, unplanned trips through rapids,

Stacked pack on top of a pack basket. Basket has shoulder straps in addition to the tumpline sharing the load.

and any number of mishaps that might occur at loading and unloading areas.

Because the pack baskets have a fixed shape, loads are easily stacked on top of them for the portages, and tumplines can be used in addition to the shoulder straps if the load is extremely heavy.

River Bags and Duffles

Before the advent of waterproof synthetic river bags, which are available in many guises and formats now, many canoeists carried their personal gear in canvas duffle bags that were lined with waterproof or water-resistant bags to shed the rain and provide safety in the event of a dunking. These duffles are still a viable means of transporting gear and can be stacked on other packs or lashed together and tumplined across the carries. If you are on a trip that will span the seasons, and canoeing will become toboggan travel, duffles are the pack of choice as they will serve a tobogganist as well as they serve a canoeist.

Army surplus outlets supplied the first rubberized bags that canoeists adapted to their uses. Then about sixteen years ago, the river supply companies began to manufacture a new generation of waterproof gear bags. A combination of scarcity of the surplus bags and improvements within the field of synthetics provided incentive for meeting the growing demands of equipment for water travelers. Northwest River Supplies of Moscow, Idaho, pioneered the first and best of these bags, which are still the most imitated by other companies.

The bags of this sort that are now standard equipment for anyone seeking truly watertight protection for clothing and sleeping bags are made from a PVC-coated Dacron that seems to stand up to the temperature extremes, excessive sun exposure, and abrasion inherent in extended canoe travel. When used with care, such gear bags often remain in serviceable condition for five or more years of hard use. Most are available in a variety of sizes and configurations and come with shoulder straps for portaging, although they can often be stacked on other systems such as wanigans or pack baskets.

Small Packs

In addition to the large bulk packs on any trip, there are likely to be a number of loose, smaller items that are convenient except when on the portage trail. Day packs for rain gear, waterproof camera cases, fishing gear, art supplies, and countless other items you want accessible all have to go somewhere. Most of the items that fall into this category are things that enhance the quality of your trip and are worth bringing along, even if they are not necessary for survival. Some can be stacked for the carries, and often as a trip progresses they can find homes in larger packs that yield more and more space as the food diminishes. A general rule of thumb for these little extras is that they are the responsibility of those for whom they are "worth it." On carries, these people will stow and carry these items without infringing on the movement of group gear.

We have discussed only some of the equipment that can be used for canoeing and portaging. It is not accidental that for the most part they are traditional items. That these items have survived a long time is evidence of their versatility, multifunctionality, and of the grace with which they fulfill all their roles on the trail. Ineffective strategies don't survive on the trail.

There are plenty of other methods, but most will not perform as well in all situations. Most also reflect a carried-over and forced-fit approach from another discipline. For example, frame packs are often seen in canoes and are great for portaging comfort but hopelessly unfit for occupying a canoe and holding enough for a canoe voyage. As a hiker's tool, they are best left on the trails.

The rafting industry uses waterproof plastic barrels for storing food and gear. Although they may fit in a canoe, provide seats in camp, and keep things dry, they are hopelessly inappropriate on the portage trail. The usual method used to carry barrels is to lash them to a pack frame. But bringing a single-purpose pack frame on a canoe trip is anathema to those who would rather delete items than add them to the load. The whole strategy is symptomatic of the gadget complex promoted by the catalog culture. Rather than back up and find an appropriate piece of gear as a solution, there is a tendency to compound inappropriateness by introducing an adaptive solution requiring the addition of some other unnecessary item.

It is an unfortunate reality of the equipment marketplace that not much of the most refined equipment is readily available. This in part explains why so many people have been forced to adapt equipment as canoe gear. Of the traditional gear I've mentioned in this chapter, only the Woods and Duluth-style packs are easily available, as are the synthetic liners and stuff sacks that make waterproofing them a simple matter.

In addition to the packs, the newer breed of waterproof gear bags are also easily available in the marketplace. Wanigans and pack baskets appeal to craftspeople who enjoy making their own equipment or are very expensive if you can find a builder. Like the finest wood and canvas canoes, these items are labor intensive and don't lend themselves to mass production.

Choice of Methods

The following section outlines my own choices for outfitting a group with equipment and the reasoning behind my choices. I encourage you to pay more attention to the thought processes that lead to the conclusions, rather than to the conclusions themselves. Each of us has different parameters shaping our choices. When two people's parameters are similar, the conclusions they draw may agree, but when their parameters differ, the conclusions drawn by one person may seem inappropriate or perhaps downright peculiar to the other.

Most of my choices result from three basic modes of travel: relatively short guided trips led by my wife, Alexandra, myself, and perhaps an apprentice; trips among peers; and solo travels. Although there is considerable overlap between the equipment I choose for each of these types of sojourns, there are also some serious differences. In all cases, however, the trips I discuss here take place in relatively wild areas where the water is drinkable, open fires are usually appropriate, and all varieties and combinations of travel and terrain are present.

The guided trips have up to six or eight paying guests who, with some exceptions, are beginners or intermediate canoeists. Most are on vacation from professional jobs and may or may not be in prime shape for the rigors of travel. These trips range from five days to two or three weeks, and meals tend toward the elaborate and surprising. Since these are vacations for the participants, high mileage, pushing limits, and overcoming odds are not high on the list of priorities. Engaging with the wilds, learning and practicing skills, and traveling in style and comfort are much more conducive to realizing a positive experience.

Given this context and a party composed of four or five canoes, the following outfit is likely. Each canoe will have one or two pack baskets for food. Each person will have one Northwest River or similar waterproof gear bag for their clothes, sleeping bag, and pad. Most people will have a small day pack, and some will have a waterproof camera case. Depending on party size, there will be one or two wanigans full of kitchen gear. The wanigans will be in those canoes that have no or just one pack basket. A Duluth-style pack that contains the rain tarps, first aid and repair kit, EPIRB or ELT (Emergency Position Indicator Radio Beacon or Emergency Location Transmitter) if one is along, field guides and other trip-related literature, and knee pads for kneeling if white water is to be encountered.

The tents will be in their own waterproof stuff bags, with one or two (if solo tents are along) distributed to each canoe. Tents are good for trimming the canoes since they can be moved around as needed, and if there is a mishap in some rapids, only a few tents will risk being lost or soaked. For the carries, however, the tents will be condensed into a single large Duluth-style pack.

If the party consists of able-bodied adults and older children, each canoe will be responsible for its load on the carries. When there are handicapped participants or children too young to provide much support to a portage, then the other members may absorb more than their share of the load. The guides and apprentices may of course do far more than their specific share, both by being in top shape for the tasks as well as being efficient through familiarity.

Generally we count on two trips per carry and, at times, more for some participants. Often the canoes are tandem carried, and people fresh out of offices may not be amused by stacked loads. Ideally, the strongest people will take one pack basket with their personal waterproof bag stacked on top of it. Day packs can be stacked or worn during a tandem canoe-carry on the second trip. The guides or apprentice will tumpline the wanigan, which will have a personal gear pack or two stacked on it. If a second wanigan is along, it may be tumped or stacked on a pack basket. Guides and apprentices will also single carry canoes.

Of course there are trips where the ideal is not met. It is here that an eclectic mix of packing strategies yields the most options. Smaller people, those who are in poor shape, and children have the option of taking very small loads, or the bulky but light loads, instead of the heavier items. Personal gear bags are generally quite light compared with food and group gear and can be carried as a full load. In the case of very small children, a day pack might be a full load. In this way, everyone assists during a carry, but only the most able deal with the heaviest elements. In such a situation, the guides or apprentice may carry a pack basket with a second one stacked on it. This might yield a load that exceeds 100 pounds if it is early in the trip, but it will free up some lighter personal bags for young people or those who are not prepared for the bigger loads. If the group has been outfitted with each canoe containing only three or four large Duluth-style packs, there would be no option for flexibility in load distribution. Many lightly loaded trips over a carry are better than risking injury and misery with over-loaded trips.

If the guided trip is a long one, the group will build up more efficiency as their skills and stamina increase. For guided trips with mixed abilities and strengths, a mix of packing strategies provides the most options, variations, and combinations for packing. Organization need not be compromised and, though Minnesotans might not like so many different items in the canoe, order and continuity can prevail.

When traveling with peers—meaning that skill, strength, stamina, and ability are relatively equal amoung trip members—the strategy could stay the same or change rather radically. The biggest factors influencing this are the size of the party and the duration of the trip. If the party is large, then a wanigan or two will still be part of the system. Pack baskets may still be chosen as the food packs, or it might be that size 3 or 4 Duluth-style or Woods packs are the food bearers. Often two people's gear can be shared in one size 4 pack, reducing the overall number of packs.

The assumption of several factors may change a few things regarding pack selection in this case. A trip of this type probably assumes (1) that all canoes will be single carried unless wind, incredibly bad terrain, or mild injury dictate otherwise and (2) that each pack load will tend toward the limits of each member's load capacity. In short, portaging will be very efficient due to each person assuming large loads, and thus the need for flexibility can be reduced or eliminated.

You may be traveling with one other person and sharing a canoe or traveling together but in solo canoes. In this case your kitchen kit won't be big enough to require a wanigan, so this can be eliminated. Elements of group gear that might require their own small pack for a large group can often be divided into personal packs on this type of trip. Food packing can take any form that is most preferred by each person, whether it be Duluth, wanigan, or pack basket. In general, the smaller the group, the easier it is to be efficient and a consummate reductionist.

When traveling solo, extreme efficiency and economy can be realized. Even for an extended sojourn, your entire outfit can probably go in a couple of Duluth-style packs, or if your venture is several months long, your food may go into additional packs. Here it is advantageous to use soft packs, as these can be rolled up and packed away when they become empty. Rigid containers of course keep their shape and occupy the same space whether in use of not. The only disadvantage of solo travel is that you are bound to make several trips per carry if your trip is of any duration, but who cares? For those who enjoy solitude, time spent on carries is of no concern anyway and is an accepted part of the bargain. Any time lost on multiple carries is repaid with dividends by the lack of time spent on group dynamics and the democratic process, which are such time-consuming aspects of group trips.

Trail Strategy

Assuming you have selected the pack types for your preferred mode of canoeing, the next step is to strategize for efficient transport during the portage. Who will carry what? How far will each pose be? How many trips will be necessary? What are the environmental constraints and their impact on the other questions?

Although it seems obvious, the need to have someone keep track of gear is often overlooked. The larger the group and the more diverse the load types, the greater the chances are that something will be left behind or that part of the group will return to the start of the trail to find nothing left to carry. Everyone has more fun if effort is not duplicated, items or people don't get lost, and everything progresses from one end of the portage to the other in an orderly manner.

A good strategy to use is to have canoers be responsible for the load in their own canoe and only help carry another canoer's gear if given permission by that other canoer. Group items might best be handled individually, such as by assigning the lunch pack to a particular person and destination. The first aid pack can always be moved forward with the first load so that when it is needed everyone can accurately predict its position without asking. A portage done by a large party in a setting where the whole distance is not covered at once might easily lead to a complete breakdown of communication as people get spread out from one another and positions and locations become confusing.

In untrailed country, the stages of a portage must be done as a group so that no members or items become lost. It is amazing how willow or spruce thickets or the vastness of the tundra can swallow up what at close range is a huge pile of stuff. More than a few puzzled portagers have had to pace off increasingly larger "boxes" around a center point while looking for a recognizable landmark that will lead them to their gear. On a gray, shadowless day, every spruce and caribou trail can look equally familiar or unfamiliar, and your distance from or ridiculous closeness to the missing gear can be very embarrassing.

With a little experience you can predict whether the carry will require one or two trips or more. This will depend on the strength of the party, the luxury level of the trip (which can affect the amount of food and other elements on the trip), and the length and roughness of the particular carry. This can change throughout a trip as the food packs get lighter and the people get stronger. In the case of a two-trip carry, each person will walk three carry lengths, two of them under load.

There is an ideal situation that experienced portagers look for wherever they travel. Every so often all the elements of the carry fall into a nice alignment that allows the one-and-a-half method to be used. Assume you have reached a point in the trip where the load has decreased to the point where there is not enough to require each person to make two full trips without one or more members carrying a ridiculously light load. Suppose also that the next carry is short enough to be done in one trip without taking any poses along the way. The trail is clear and each canoe pulls up and unloads. Your partner takes the canoe all the way to water at the far end. Meanwhile, you take a load of packs to the estimated halfway point and put them down. You return to the start, get the final load, and start back. Just about the time that you arrive at the halfway spot, your partner, who took the canoe all the way, arrives there from the opposite direction. Your partner then picks up the first load of packs and you both proceed to the distant end. Each of you will have walked one full trip under load, one half-trip with no load, and one half-trip with load, for a total distance of only two carry lengths. You both arrive at the canoe at the same time and can embark easily and quickly. Those parties that don't know this trick will be busy with a third carry trip while you slip away with glee.

There are myriad other tricks that can ease your passage on the carries. In general, balance is more important than strength, especially when flipping up canoes or getting a tumped wanigan settled comfortably. Despite technique and balance, the initial lifting of a load is the most energy draining aspect of a carry. Enlist irregular terrain, trees, boulders, slopes, your companions, and even your other gear to help you save energy.

When you carry a stacked load, it is easier to have a companion assist you by handing you the second pack or by giving you a hand to reduce the stress of

Rising from terrain assisted lifting of load.
Roots and rock in immediate background
provide an elevated platform from which to
raise the load. Ax has been placed for easy
retrieval without bending over.

Single carried canoe at rest stage; tandem
carried canoe in background.

a one-legged deep-knee bend as you try to rise after a fall or from deep mud. If someone is there at the end, they can assist in unloading or stabilizing a canoe in a high wind.

If there is a steep bank or a flat-topped boulder, you might be able to slip into a pack or tumpline without having to lift and swing the load up. If there is a crotched tree or two trees close together, you may be able to rest by wedging the bow of the canoe in the notch and stepping out from underneath it rather than by putting down the canoe and getting it back up by a full flip. Of course there will be plenty of times when no one is around and you are on flat treeless terrain, but that should not stop you from being an opportunist when conditions permit it.

Aside from choosing pack types and making the best use of people and terrain in your planning, there is that final element of the portage that comes down to doing hard work under heavy loads. Under extreme loading you will find that you always time your breathing to the same rhythm of pace and trail. Regardless of whether there are blowdowns, mud, loose rocks, boulders, or good footing, you will find that a shuffle that is faster than a walk and slower than a trot is most comfortable. You can do this best with slightly sprung knees, which can absorb all the shocks of irregular ground. Under an extreme load, a locked knee and a straight leg can be a complete liability, as nothing but bone on bone and your ligaments will absorb the shock should you slip in that position.

Your final refinements in the art of portaging will come from your ability to understand your group, the difficulty of the terrain, and how you balance these factors when arriving at a strategy for load moving. With beginners, many trips with light loads will preserve a high energy level, avoid fatigue-related stress or injury, and ease people into the routines of carrying. Such an approach takes time due to the greater distance walked. As your party grows more familiar with portaging as a trip progresses, and stronger through repeated carries, you can alter your approach.

At some point you might load heavier and take shorter poses along the carry route. If a quarter mile is as far as your load allows you before agony sets in, stop there. Rest on the return trip for the second load. Repeat this leapfrogging of gear along the trail until you reach your destination. The short poses will preserve your energy and comfort by reducing stress, and frequent short rests are better than long ones. The terrain will tell you when poses are appropriate. On a portage that is high, dry, and flat, you might go a long way before taking a pose. If the ground is excessively steep, bouldery, and bedeviled with blowdowns, you might get only 100 yards before collapsing at a pose. Some carries have sections that are so rough that a cooperative effort by the whole party is required to lower gear down ledges and cliffs or to coax it up out of ravines and canyons.

At times where footing and slope are fine, the wind may be a problem, particularly to the person carrying the canoe. In such a situation the pack carrier will have to walk behind the canoe to stabilize it from one end. This courtesy prevents the canoe carrier from being gyrated around like a crashing helicopter. If rough ground is an additional part of this equation, the passage is anything but easy.

Oftentimes a portage is encountered at a time of day when camp can be made at one end or the other. This offers a number of options for distributing the work over two different days. It may be that only the supper and breakfast packs and personal gear and tents need to go over to insure a comfortable camp at the far end. After supper the ambitious might bring some other gear part or all the way across, and the rest can be done in the morning when everyone is fresh. Some very long portages may require one or more overnights along them anyway, and here the benefits of skillful organization and effective delegation of respomsibilities—who moves what, and where and when—will pay off in the extreme.

Portaging is the final ace up the canoeist's sleeve. This skill alone allows passage anywhere to everyone. Trips on rough, raggedy, woolly rivers are not just the province of those skilled in white water. Another passport to the same country could just as well be the skills of the carry, which likewise serve as keys to the country back of beyond.

Considered choices for equipment and technique reveal many options. Think about them clearly and carefully, and strive for economy of means. You can then apply the energy you save to those elements of the trip that are much more fun than portaging—elements that probably lured you into such remarkable country in the first place.

Much Ado About the Tumpline: Making the Unpleasant Bearable

A survey of load-carrying methods used around the world would reveal two recurring observations. Those cultures with the best methods make the most use of the human skeleton in relation to musculature, and almost all cultures use a tumpline in one form or another to assume part or all of the load. Groups who do not use a tumpline usually represent one of the so-called civilized cultures, and they would have one too if their history of getting other people to do their load carrying wasn't so long.

The age of machinery has done much to reduce the need for human-carried loads, but where the terrain gets too rough or too wet for elephants, camels, yaks, horses, llamas, jeeps, skidders, and ATVs, then you find people shouldering whatever needs to be moved. From equatorial jungles to the barrens of the high Arctic, almost every native culture has a form of tumpline.

In North America the native people passed on knowledge of the tumpline to those who had occasion to fan out across the continent in search of exploitable resources. Among the least ethnocentric of the colonizers were the French voyageurs who adopted the finer points of native woodcraft and mobility in the wilds. Although the voyageurs mostly performed as high-speed transcontinental transport toilers for the fur companies, their history, exploits, and songs are close to the hearts of many a modern wilderness canoeist. And the voyageurs are a direct link in history to those cultures that have contributed so much to the evolution of modern canoeing knowledge and technique, including the tumpline tradition.

The tumpline is a remarkably simple piece of equipment. It consists of a wide band for the headpiece and of tails of varying lengths that are tied to a load, which is then carried snug against the carrier's back and borne by the headpiece, which passes over the head just where the crown merges into the forehead. Properly adjusted, the device rests on the nice thick frontal portion of the skull and by its very nature lines up all the vertebrae and relies on the long bones of the legs to support the load. A slight forward lean puts all the forces in line with the skeleton, which supports most of the weight. This leaves a person's musculature free to engage in a springy stride that allows for both shock-absorption and forward motion. Although the tumpline itself may weigh only a few ounces, it allows the carrying of phenomenal loads that beggar one's sense of credibility.

A voyageur was typically under contract to carry two 90-pound "pieces" simultaneously on each trip over a portage. Most voyageurs were not large people, and these bandy legged souls who may have weighed in at 135 or 140 pounds were obliged to lug 180 pounds each trip. Being exuberant and competitive, many of them tended to carry more than that for glory, to outdo someone, or for fun. Five pieces (450 pounds) was not an uncommon record on some carries. The frequency of ruptures and death by strangulated hernia seem to corroborate such figures.

Impressive as those figures might be in the context of commerce on the portages, the figures for competition are much higher. Granted, most competitions involve staggering 40 feet, turning around, and staggering back to the starting point. All but the winners lose it trying to make the corner. At the summer games in the Cree village of Mistassini, Quebec, women have carried close to 900 pounds and men have exceeded 1,200. The same is true at native games all over the North from Inuit communities near Point Barrow to the shores of Hudson Bay.

A study conducted by the United States Army found that load bearers who rely on the skeleton either by direct head loading, as done by some African cultures, or by tumpline, can carry 25 pounds "free" before burning a single extra calorie for the work. Foot soldiers carrying packs with shoulder straps begin burning calories almost instantly.

As a canoeist, my personal level of comfort under a tumpline falls off sharply at about 100 pounds. Even though I can carry much more than that doesn't mean I want to or will. Usually I can avoid carrying more than 90 pounds. Depending on the terrain and trail, or lack of trail, I can go a quarter to a half mile or more before taking a pose and then "resting" while I walk back empty for another load. With a shoulder-strap load, my comfort threshold falls off well below 60 pounds; this may be a rough corroboration of the 25 "free"-pound figure determined by the Army researchers.

Anyone who learns to use a tumpline well will never go back to other methods. Two difficulties with tumplines are their lack of general availability and the time investment required to become familiar, indeed fluent, with their use. You have to make your own to solve the first problem, and you need to be taught to use one in person in order to maximize the potential of the learning process.

If you are a Duluth-style pack user, you are in luck. Many of these packs, such as the Superior pack system, come with adjustable tumplines as optional features. For canoe carrying, wanigan carrying, or tumping combined duffles, however, you need a bit of patience and know-how. Once the system is perfected and understood, and becomes second nature, the carries of canoe country will be more bearable than you might dare imagine. They will never be fun, but an increment of increased ease is worth a lot when the bugs are thick, the muskeg deep, and the way obscure. Such gains are worth a lot even on a wide-open, short, dry, easy portage.

Canoeists' tumplines are infinitely variable, but an average one might consist of a 22-inch-long, $2^1/_4$-inch-wide headpiece riveted or sewn to two 9- or 10-

foot tails that might be $^3/_4$ of an inch wide and may or may not taper toward the ends. Typically they are of a well oiled leather, though canvas or nylon are often used as a headpiece with rope, leather, or webbing for the tails. Climbers' webbing has been suggested as a good material, and I would like to try it. My one reservation has to do with the ease with which I could undo the knots at the load-bearing points. Slippery nylon has a way of tightening on itself over the jolty long haul, and I much prefer knots that can be undone over those that inspire tantrums and explosions of exasperated cursing.

In Canada, the use of the tumpline among wilderness canoeists is still quite prevalent. In the Lower 48, almost anyone knowledgeable in their use has either been a camper or counselor at one of the great famed canoe camps of the Temagami region or knew someone who was.

There seem to be two very rigid viewpoints held by those who know of tumplines at all. The zealots worship them as mystical, gravity defying devices. When they meet as perfect strangers on some obscure carry halfway across Ontario, they clasp each other like long-lost descendants of an extinct tribe.

As far as I can tell there is no middle ground of ambivalence. You never hear anyone musing, "Oh tumplines, yeah, I can take 'em or leave 'em."

The opposing opinion sounds more like this: "Tumplines! You gotta be kidding. Those are torture devices. Notch-heads are the only folks who'd use 'em. Ya know what a notch-head is? It's someone who's deformed by too many loads squishing their brains out on the carry trails…" The tirade lasts a lot longer than that; the only way to stop it is to wander off. I doubt anyone has actually ever witnessed the concluding remarks of a nontumper.

My guess is that those who are vehemently opposed to the tumpline are those who have used one without taking the time to fine-tune and ensure a proper fit. This is the fussiest point in the tumpline equation and requires some patience and experimentation to get it right. If one never experiences getting things right, then the anguished howling and abject misery is easy to sympathize with and is entirely justifiable. A tumpline adjusted even a fraction of an inch too long or too short is indeed aggravating beyond belief.

The easiest tumplines to adjust are those that are part of the Duluth-style or Woods packs. Typically these are adjustable by means of tails that pass through a roller buckle on a short strap sewn to the pack. With several holes in the tump tails from which to choose, you can adjust the fit quickly and easily. In a pinch, a new hole can be punched between the others to ensure a precise fit. Most people adopt a half-and-half distribution of weight between shoulder straps and tumpline.

Adjustment becomes more fussy and precise for loads that are completely carried by the tumpline and not distributed via shoulder straps. The canoe, wanigans, and bundled soft-packs or duffles are in this category. All are adjusted by means of a knot being placed with precision. Once tied off, the only means of adjustment is to untie and shift the placement of the load-bearing knots. This, of course, takes time and means putting down and fixing the load. If adjustment is required, do it. It takes a few minutes to do, but this is always preferable to the many minutes or hours of agony that result from portaging with a system that is not adjusted precisely enough. Don't let impatient comrads or thick bugs fool you into scampering along the trail with an ill-adjusted load. The penalty for such false economy is never worth it.

Tumping a canoe relies on fixed knots on the center thwart, but if you are using paddles with tapered instead of flat-sided blades for the carrying yoke, then the tumpline is, in fact, adjustable en route without putting down the canoe.

In keeping with the strategy of using multifunctional gear as an approach to reducing the overall load, I prefer to use paddles as a portage yoke. Since paddles have to be carried over the portages anyway, why not make them work for their passage and make their weight valuable? Place paddles over the center thwart and the tumpline over each paddle face with the headstrap falling between them where the carrier's head goes. The width of the paddles where the line crosses determines how tight or loose the line is and what portion of the load is on the paddles and shoulders and what is on the tumpline and head. Northwoods paddles taper evenly from their widest section of blade to where the shaft begins. By sliding the paddles forward (widening the blade), or sliding them back (narrowing the blade), you can tighten or add slack to the tumpline. This little trick allows several inches of adjustment.

In general, most people select a half-and-half adjustment for the weight of the canoe, but occasionally an en route "rest" can be taken by shifting the proportion of weight borne by shoulders or tumpline. In addition, if the adjustment is not quite precise, or if different people are taking shifts carrying the canoe, it is often possible to compensate without adjusting the knots.

Canoe rigged for portage with paddles as carrying yoke, and tumpline set to take half the weight.

There is a wonderful rule of thumb that seems to work for most people when it comes to adjusting tumplines accurately. In fact, it may be one of the only rules of thumb where one's thumb actually figures into the process. If you have never tumped a load before and have no idea how to figure out the proper length from headpiece to load-bearing knots, the following method will get you very close.

In the case of a canoe, rig your paddles to provide a yoke, or if you have a padded carrying bar, as the Minnesotans prefer, kneel down beside your canoe and place your elbow on the center of the thwart or carrying bar. Extend the thumb of that hand, which is a forearm's length above the thwart, and hang the center of the tumpline headpiece over it. Take one tail and place it outboard of the paddles or pads on the yoke or thwart. At that point, tie off the tumpline tail. Once that is done, repeat the thumb and elbow trick to determine where the remaining tail should be tied off. This will be within a few inches of proper adjustment. Flip the canoe up into carrying position and note if the tumpline is too tight or too loose. Adjust accordingly until the load distribution is half and half or whatever you prefer. Once this adjustment is made, slip your thumb under the tump and see where your elbow or forearm falls on the thwart. Remember this position and never forget it. Thereafter you will know your exact reference point and will no longer need to experiment.

One other factor affects this adjustment. When carrying a canoe, I wear my

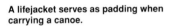

A lifejacket serves as padding when carrying a canoe.

lifejacket as padding at the paddle-bearing points and have selected one with foam panels that go over the top of my shoulders. Since the lifejacket has to cross the carry anyway, I choose to make it work for its passage. This means I have to accommodate the thickness of the padding in the tumpline length adjustment. In my case this means that my elbow encounters the thwart not at the point but at the little notch a few inches farther up my forearm.

For carrying a wanigan or bundled soft-packs, the rule of thumb for me is that starting with the point of my elbow on the top surface of the load will result in a comfortable adjustment. If I wish to increase the load by stacking other packs, these will be stacked on top of the wanigan and extend above my neck and head, thus leaving the load-bearing knots in the tumpline in a fixed position at about shoulder level.

One additional note is that the tie points for wanigans should be spaced widely enough so that the tumpline tails do not chafe your shoulders but pass to the outside, exerting no pressure on shoulder bones or muscles.

In the case of tumping a wanigan or a wanigan and stacked additional load, the adjustment of tumpline length must be precise. Too tight and your head and neck will be pulled back. This is agonizingly uncomfortable because your neck muscles hold the load rather than a nice chiropractically correct alignment of neck and back disks. If the adjustment is too loose you will get the infamous *wanigan bite*, a term coined in the Temagami region of Ontario. A wanigan bite results from the hard bottom edge of the wanigan digging in to the big muscles in the small of your back, creating an excruciating sore on the muscles or the nubbins of whichever unlucky disk in your back gets bitten. Either of these problems is enough to inspire accurate adjustment. In addition, if it is not unbearably hot on the carry, you can wear a lifejacket and let the foam panels absorb a would-be wanigan bite; this will also move the lifejacket to the appropriate end of the carry.

Several misinformed writers have stated that the tumpline can be dangerous in a fall. Usually falls are at least partially caused by extremely difficult footing. Falls may occur when crossing blowdowns, boulders, extremely steep or brushy terrain, or any and all conceivable combinations of these, often with wind as a factor. In such cases your feet, ankles, and legs are at far greater risk than your neck and head. A fall with a shoulder-strap load means you are going all the way down with the load, and you hope your feet and legs are free because the weight of the load is going to be added to your body weight and the leverage on your long bones increased.

In all of the tumpline falls I've experienced, I have been able to release the load and in many cases get it off and stabilized so quickly and well that I recovered my balance and never suffered a full-body landing.

Theoretically the canoe is probably the most confining load. You have paddles or a yoke on each side of your neck, a thwart behind your neck, and a tight line over the top of your head. All of this may be in a giant wind vane if you are in the open. If you simply drop your head forward, the tumpline comes off to the rear, your head is safely below the level of the paddle blades, and the canoe can be rolled in the direction you are falling or to the downslope side if you are on a sidehill. Always fall on the canoe if you can, rather than letting it fall on you. In many cases you can put the canoe down in a manner that holds you up and you never consummate a loss of balance with a full fall.

With wanigans or other loads, dipping your head and rolling your body will spill the load in a controlled direction even as you fall. Again, try to release on the downhill side or in the direction of the fall. Always lose the load to save your body. Damaged equipment is easily and quickly fixed overnight in camp. Damaged bones, muscles, and ligaments and abrasions from falling require time that may not be available for healing and rebuilding.

Given a choice, I'd rather slip out of a tumpline than be dragged down by shoulder straps.

Not only will fluent use of tumplines ease your way across the trails of canoe country, but at night in camp the lines can be pressed into service to air sleeping bags, dry things after that week of rainy weather, or be a guy for a kitchen tarp. It would be a shame to leave 18 or 20 perfectly good feet of tumpline lying around doing nothing, despite the fact that such a hard-working, high-yield piece of equipment may deserve a rest for performing any one of its functions.

The most complete discussion of how-to information about the tumpline appears in Heb Evans's book *Canoeing Wilderness Water*, 1975, A. S. Barnes and Co., Inc., Cranbury, NJ. It is out of print and difficult to find, but libraries may have it. G. Heberton Evans was a long-time associate of the Keewaydin Camps of Temagami, and his books reveal the Keewaydin way of extended travel. Most elements are well presented despite the presence of some techniques that are not the best. Overall they are great books with better than usual notes on traditional expertise.

Encountering Ice

5

While my first venture into canoe country of the North lasted three and one half months, most subsequent returns to the wilderness were longer—as long as I could afford. Trip followed trip, in no set pattern. Season overlapped season; sometimes a canoe was hauled in by dog-sled or toboggan, or a toboggan was hauled in by canoe.
North American Canoe Country, *Calvin Rutstrum -1964*

Thus far we have looked at elements of the work- and travel-canoe cultures that pride themselves on achieving streamlined ease and efficiency. For the most part, the refinements of design and technique involve equipment that has multiple functions and can span a range of conditions. There is one item in the northwoods outfit, however, that remains extremely specialized. Not only is the item good for only two things, but the portion of the canoeing season when it can be used is limited. That item is the ice hook.

An ice hook is indispensable just before freeze-up in the fall and during ice-out in the spring. Its two uses: getting from hard ice to open water and getting from open water to hard ice. Both processes are most pleasant when neither cargo nor people get wet. Icy water is notoriously unsympathetic to warm-blooded creatures such as canoeists.

The two best ice hooks available are a pulp logger's hookeroon with a 4-foot handle or, better yet, something called an ice hook, which was used in the days before refrigeration when lake ice was stored in ice houses for use during the summer. Ice hooks of this sort still exist in antique shops and come with

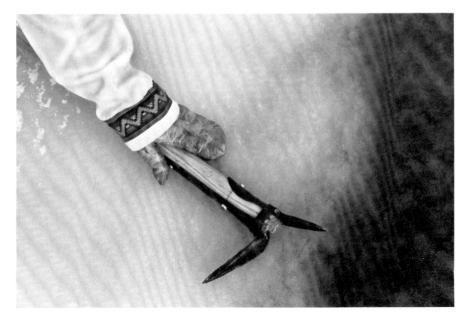

Business end of ice-house style ice hook showing the hook and spud. The white ice under the hook is older ice, and the black ice to the right of the point on the spud is newer and thinner ice.

4- and 6-foot handles. The 4-foot handle is the most appropriate for canoe usage and is also the easiest to find in old tool shops. The beauty of the ice-house-style hook is that it has not only a recurved hook piece but also a short spud on the end that is useful for testing ice thickness, improving your stability while walking on ice, and allowing you to push the canoe as if you were poling. Haunt the antique shops for these, and if that fails get a hookeroon from a forestry supply catalog or axe company.

In the northern tier of the lower 48 states, shelf ice is likely to form in coves and quiet sections where the water is still anytime after November 1. By December, travel without an ice hook is a foolhardy venture and remains so until the last crack freezes over and ice travel becomes possible. In the spring the rivers break up as much as a month before the lakes are free of the last gray and rotting ice. At either time the temperature of the water is such that survival time is compressed into a matter of minutes in the event of full immersion. Correct use of an ice hook coupled with respectful caution and applied knowledge provide a safe way to encounter the vagaries caused by fall turning to winter and winter turning to spring.

Fall Ice

Fall ice has properties of structure and strength that make it the easiest to understand and consistent enough for a few basic rules to usually hold true. For example, 1 inch of black "fall ice" will hold a person, 2 inches are safe, 6 inches will hold a horse, 8 a team, and so on up to the driving of vehicles and the landing of aircraft. In the far North, temporary winter roads and even railroads will cross lakes directly rather than follow the long summer routes that must circumnavigate huge bodies of water and muskeg.

Fall ice describes the very clear ice that results from a quick freeze that incorporates little in the way of trapped gas bubbles or snow, which is what makes older or metamorphosed ice appear gray or white. "Black ice" is another term for it. It is the most elastic and resilient form of ice and has maximum tensile strength. Even the clearest fast-freeze ice will reveal tiny gas bubbles trapped within it, and these are arranged in vertical trails. By lying on the ice and shielding your eyes from reflection and glare, you can see these and thereby gauge the thickness of the sheet. Better yet, stress cracks that form where ice expands when building and shrinks from extreme cold will show you the thickness with a much more visible edge in view. The interface along such a crack will reflect light and appear white. A glance at such a crack will tell you if you have a foot of ice or a few inches or if it would be wise to retreat.

It is worth finding an area that you know is shallow and waiting for that first ice-forming cold snap in the late fall. If your visits coincide with the initial ice forming, you can learn a great deal by testing and observation. You will find that $3/_4$ of an inch of ice may hold you even though it sags several inches and a webwork of cracks radiates from the epicenter of each placement of weight. It may be that, with feet together, you break through and that with feet spread in the manner of polar bears and the Inuit you stay aloft. Fall ice generally takes a few seconds to sag and completely break through. In this time span between warning and breakage, you can often retreat or redistribute your weight to a more advantageous position.

In such a manner you can learn an enormous amount for the very modest price of cold shins and maybe a boot full of cold water. The elastic thin ice does not last long if the weather continues cold. On a clear night with no wind and maximum radiational cooling, another inch of ice may make up. If you have access to a larger body of water that doesn't cool so quickly, you can witness the remarkable plasticity of the early ice. If the main lake is open and a smaller bay is just skimming over, you can actually see greatly elongated waves moving through the ice as wind-generated waves from the open water encounter the increased surface tension of the new ice sheet. If the ice is strong enough to support you, it is possible to feel the subtle undulations through your feet after the waves cease to be visible as the ice approaches an inch in thickness.

Test all ice encountered. Then retest it. Apply your ever-expanding body of knowledge but refrain from thinking that you know ice. Never completely trust the rules or yourself. With time and exposure to the infinite variety of ice and situations, you will develop many skills and perhaps even a sixth sense of what is safe and what is not. Be exploratory and calculating and pay attention to intuition. Check things out at the slightest provocation—a subtle creeping cold between the shoulder blades, erect hairs at the base of the neck, a sudden lack of deer and fox tracks on the ice, your dog stopping. Clues will come in many guises and it doesn't take long to check them out, especially compared to how long it takes to dry out and warm up from a mistake. One or two blows with an axe, ice chisel, or the spud of an ice hook will tell you if the minimum 2 inches for safety exists or not.

Trust your fear in combination with your common sense and constantly explore, chip, prod, break, and study ice. Despite the basic guidelines, all ice is variable and influencing conditions are often subtle. A dusting of new snow can hide the visual clues that might indicate an under-ice current or spring keeping an area thin or the presence of a recently frozen open lead. Be aware that you may be playing a game without being privy to all the rules and conditions.

With the confidence gained from shallow water experiments and study, you may decide that the time has come to venture off into that hidden marsh or a section of wild river seldom visited in late fall. Let us assume there are 20 feet of ice between shore and open water at the put-in. The first 8 feet are old ice and have been there several days. They are opaque and frosty because of a little snow incorporated in the upper layers. The ice responds to a sharp blow with a solid thump, and you suspect it is sound. By chipping through you find it is 4 inches thick.

The new ice is nearly clear as glass and you can see water weeds green as salad waving in the current below. You can also see from a stress crack that runs to the ice edge at open water that the new ice tapers evenly from 3 inches at the interface with the old ice to nothing at waterside.

Place the canoe on the solid ice pointing directly toward the open water at right angles to the ice edge. Any gear should be placed in positions that will yield proper trim once the canoe is afloat (no gear if this is introductory experimentation and practice).

If there are two people, you must decide which method of approach has the most appeal. Old-timers are equally divided between those who favor having canoeists on the same or opposite sides of the canoe when approaching open water; my own experience has not yet indicated if one or the other is more effective.

Both lines of reasoning address the possibility of a simultaneous breakthrough as the ice edge is reached. The same-siders feel that entering the canoe from a common side is easier because the weight transfer from feet-on-ice to hands-on-rails will depress the near rail slightly and facilitate both feet clearing the rail to settle into the canoe. The opposite-siders feel that greater stability prevails because the canoe will not tip at all if weight transferal from opposite sides cancels any tendency to tip. Having used both methods, and never having suffered a breakthrough, I still have no actual reference on which to base a choice. Both scenarios seem right to me, and perhaps they are. If one method was less effective than the other, I doubt that each would coexist equally as techniques espoused by experienced old-timers.

Regardless of which method yields the most confidence, the physical techniques remain the same whether you are on opposite sides of the canoe or the same. Each of you will lean over and grasp opposite gunnels at a point that is wide enough to ensure stability. The stern person should take care to be far enough forward so that if the canoe must be entered suddenly, no interference is caused by the stern seat or the narrowing of the stern.

In this somewhat awkward stance, ease the canoe forward while maintaining the potential for instant transferal of weight to the gunnels and canoe. As the bow person eases out onto the thinner ice, more and more weight will be shifted to the gunnels, leaving only enough on the feet to maintain traction. The larger surface area of the canoe will allow you to "walk" on some incredibly thin ice. At this point the ice will depress, and usually it will sink enough so that water will run up on top of it. This of course lubricates the ice; while you lose your traction potential, the water improves the canoe's sliding potential.

At this point the bow person will smoothly transfer all their weight through their arms to the rails and will spring their feet lightly into the canoe. Kneeling in the bow at this point will increase the stability of the canoe both on ice and in

1

2

3

4

Approaching the ice edge tandem. Bow person eases out toward ice edge (1) while maintaining stance on rails for instant weight transfer to canoe (2). At thin depressable ice (3), the bow gets in and braces for stability once over water (4), while stern person continues to edge of weak ice and enters also (5).

5

the water.

On good ice, the canoe, with its large surface area, will still be on the ice. The stern person will usually be on much thicker ice and can, in fact, continue toward the ice edge with the same readiness for weight transferal that the bow person maintained. The farther the canoe is pushed, the more the ice will sag; it may be that the bow will begin to break through the thin ice at the edge and, if not, may simply slide off into the open water. Beneath the canoe is a sloped trough lubricated with water that has flowed up on it. The stern person can then judge when it is best to get in—or may be inspired to get in by the ice giving up. In most cases the canoe slides into the water on its own.

In the event that the slide does not take place, or the canoe breaks through before reaching open water, there are a couple of options. If the ice hook has a spud bit as well as a hook, the stern person can push off the good ice from behind. The bow person may have enough water to paddle forward and assist in this way, or there may be large enough ice pans for the bow person to pull with the hook from the front. In shallow water it may be possible to pole with the hook, paddles, or a setting pole from the bottom.

At this point it is a good idea to return to the edge at the entry point and examine the thickness at waterside, a few feet back, where breakthrough seemed imminent, and where the last of the solid footing tapered to less than that.

The return from open water to hard ice is slightly more difficult and requires a bit more judgment and knowledge of the ice. In going from hard ice to water you can get into the canoe too early, which is always safe. But too early an exit from the canoe when going from water to ice is never safe. The bow person should always attempt to go several feet beyond known safety before testing the ice for weight placement beside the canoe.

This process is essentially the reverse of the other with the addition of a few details. In approaching the ice, the bow person should move enough gear aft so that he or she can occupy the space just behind the bow seat. This placement of gear and bow person ensures a trim that will raise the bow out of the water enough for the canoe to ride up over the edge of the ice. If the ice is at all breakable, the canoe will break down through it ice-breaker fashion. Never try to approach or break ice by butting it from water level. It won't work and you might damage the canoe.

At the point where pole- or paddle-power from the stern fails to move the canoe any farther onto the ice, the stern person should assume a low brace position with the paddle in deep water or should brace with the pole in the shallows to increase stability. The bow person will then reach ahead and set the ice hook with the handle close to the edge of the canoe and parallel to the intended direction of pull. This ensures a direct pull and minimizes any tendency for the canoe to pivot. A steady pull moves the canoe forward onto the ice, usually with the benefit of lubrication due to water flowing up on the depressed ice.

In an ideal situation, the ice tapers evenly until it is thick enough to support the canoeists' weight when they step out of the canoe. In such a case the bow person might actually pull the canoe all the way up onto the ice and reach a position of assured safety with no resistance.

However, it is more likely that the ice edge will be composed of ice of different ages or that suddenly tapers from thin to thick. In this case, there will be a point where the ice is thick enough to resist being depressed and instead will

exert pressure on the hull due to the weight in it and the decreasing support from the water. In a wood and canvas canoe you can see the ribs and planking flexing; in a synthetic canoe the inward bulge is even more pronounced. The point where this pressure becomes critical is usually just ahead of the center thwart in an empty canoe and in the region of the forward quarter-thwart in a loaded canoe. At this point do not force the canoe any farther forward; you will reduce remaining stability, and the weight in the unsupported bow is becoming too great.

   Ice that is too thick to be depressed by the weight of the canoe can also reveal that it is safe for the bow person to consider getting out. After testing the ice alongside the canoe, the bow person may prepare to get out by grasping

Following the testing and exiting conducted by the bow person, the canoe is stabilized while the stern person moves forward over the load to safe ice, and both then tow the canoe to solid ice.

opposite gunnels and placing one foot on the ice next to the canoe. By slowly weighting the outboard foot, the safety of the ice will be revealed while complete safety is maintained. The hands on gunnels and the foot still in the canoe are all ready for instant weight transfer at the slightest hint of weak ice.

Assuming all is well, you have the choice of pushing the canoe ahead scooter-style with one foot still in it or of letting the other foot join the first on the ice. With your weight still largely supported by your hands on the gunnels, you can then proceed forward with the same readiness to reenter the canoe should anything go wrong. This readiness involves the same stance and techniques as when going from hard ice to water, only your direction has changed.

With the bow person out of the canoe, the stern sinks a little deeper but can still be pulled forward before ice pressure on the hull is such that it should go no further. With the bow person steadying the craft, the stern person is free to move forward over the load and exit at the bow. It is then a simple matter to tow the canoe all the way up onto the hard ice.

Spring Ice

Spring ice is entirely different in nature and structure. Thaws, refreezings, and general decomposition make it treacherous. Hair-trigger wits, a lot of experience, and extreme care should accompany anyone who leaves shore.

There are two major reasons for the additional danger associated with spring ice. Both are related to the process of thawing. Spring ice loses the tensile strength and plasticity that characterize fall ice; and its surface often becomes slushy and granular, eliminating any visual clues to structure, thickness, and strength.

The decomposition process takes place in a manner that weakens the vertical structure of the ice. The ice, in effect, becomes a sheet composed of perpendicular columns all packed together but with extremely limited shear strength between columns. "Honeycomb" and "candle" ice are colloquial names, and each is a good description of the look and size of the columns. Because the shear strength between the adjacent columns is limited, it is possible for blocks of ice to give way like pieces of a jigsaw puzzle. No longer do thickness guidelines apply. Unlike fall ice, which creaks, sags, and gives up slowly, spring ice lets go suddenly and without warning. This is just as likely to occur with ice up to a foot or more thick as it is with thin ice.

Decomposition varies radically with the amount of heat, wind, evaporation, rain, and other weather-related events. Should this be coupled with periods of refreezing and rethawing, the structure is further altered.

There is only one visual clue to the relative stages of thaw. If the ice is white, and this may actually be the slush and granular snow over the true ice, it may be safe. Test it. If the surface is gray and rotten looking, it is saturated with water and in an advanced stage of decomposition. Stay away from it. If there is any wind or wave action farther out in the open water, you should be able to hear the tinkle of the once-verticle candles and honeycombs falling over and floating horizontally at the ice edge.

The techniques for entry and exit are the same regarding the canoe and the use of the hook. It is your care and caution that must be maintained at a nervewracking pitch when on the uncertain ice of spring or on the summer ice of the Barren Grounds.

With experience, deliberate and continuous study, and sound common sense, you can extend the canoeing season significantly. If you are on a long trip and do not want to carry a full ice hook with a long handle all summer, you can remove the iron hook and spud elements and carry only them. When the need arises for the ice hook, you can then fashion a handle for it. If you travel beyond the timber you will need to bring handle stock, but even this can be converted to firewood once the ice-hooking requirements are no longer necessary.

Whereas the ice hook is a tool that is useful in an environment where there is water and some ice, or for the transition from partly open water to full-fledged ice, the canoe sled is something that comes into use when the proportion of overland or ice travel takes dominance over the remaining open water. For those who work in the woods during transition seasons, or who will be traveling great distances during the shift from fall to winter, permanent or temporary canoe sleds may join your arsenal of equipment.

In the days before bush flights, snowmobiles, and road proliferation, the canoe sled was familiar to hunters, trappers, surveyors, timber cruisers, and anyone who by choice or contract lived in the bush through the fall and into winter. Like many other bush skills that were at one time part of everyday knowledge, the traditions of canoe sled usage are being revived by modern recreational travelers who want to experience longer engagements with the wilds, often including the transitions between seasons.

In the archives of the Geological Survey of Canada there is a picture of A. P. Low and four Montagnais guides on the ice of Winokapau Lake in Labrador. Behind them is a Peterborough or Chestnut canoe on a runnered sled. It is the spring of 1894. In the 1930s another geologist, E. P. Wheeler, was roaming the Labrador Plateau country. His research trips were each eighteen months in duration. To maximize the use of each summer, he would winter over, and with much or his work dependent on outcrops and exposed ledges, could continue work even in the snow months when the wind kept his sites free of snow. A Chestnut canoe and a sled of his own design were consistent parts of his outfit.

In addition to researchers, countless trappers and families of hunters were on the land all across the North, and even today it is not unusual to find a sled cached in the trees or secured in a spruce-pole shelter at some convenient junction of rivers or where a winter trail leaves a water route and strikes out over land.

Renowned Maine Guide Mick Fahey once told me of one late fall when he

Canoe Sleds

Canoe and freight sled made and used by E. P. Wheeler in conducting geological research in the 1930s.

and another guide were desperately trying to paddle out of the woods on the last possible day ahead of freeze-up. Slush was forming in the water from a storm that was dumping a foot of snow on the ground. They had paddled about 20 miles of lake when the slush ice was forming up thick enough to stop them. Five hundred miles to the north of the two guides, the term would have been "slob ice;" in the middle of Maine, Mick and his partner just swore at it as it thickened around them and compared it to porridge and cement. Although both were young men at the time, they weren't lacking in the necessary savvy of the season and each had a 7-foot runnered sled in his canoe.

When the slush finally seized them, they were ready. Each had a 20-foot E. M. White canoe, and the center thwart had a pair of wing nuts rather than hex nuts holding it in place. This was a distinct advantage when carrying around moose or deer or moose sleds, or for sleeping in canoes. With the center thwart removed, there was nearly 6 feet of clear space between the quarter thwarts. It was likely that when the storm cleared it would get cold and, with luck, by dawn the slush ice would permit travel as it would build up faster and thicker than if the slowly increasing cold were building ice layer by layer. The slush provided substance and plenty of molecules for the cold to weld together.

By dark the gear had been rearranged into the ends of the canoes and the midsections prepared as sleeping platforms with extra clothing and blankets as insulation. The men reclined in their sleeping bags smoking their pipes and watching the weather. When the snow stopped and a fleet of brittle stars appeared, they smiled. Once arranged, they stretched a tarp over the two canoes to keep their own heat from radiating away and slept until dawn. Luck was with them. They could walk on the ice. They chopped out the canoes and switched the roles of sled and boat. Now the sled carried the canoe and a pair of gingerly stepping men pulled the sleds with their tumplines.

The canoe sled provides two services. It protects the hull from sharp and irregular rough ice and, when over land, from rocks, stumps, and discontinuities that might inflict damage. Of equal importance, it also vastly reduces friction by decreasing the bearing area of a large hull to the surface area of two narrow runners. If a canoe is placed upright on a sled, cradled securely, and filled with the gear that would normally be in it, the load is usually fairly easy to handle either by tandem pulling or by shifting off now and then when being pulled singly. Steep terrain can of course require taking partial loads and working extra hard, but if most of the route sticks to the ice and the lowest ground between watersheds, travel can be a joy.

In Maine there were moose sleds that were 7 or 8 feet long and had shod spruce runners and a flat bed. They were utility sleds made to haul anything and everything and were serviceable enough to eclipse the use of the Indian-style toboggans for general travel purposes. That they were called upon at times to haul canoes was as natural as hauling wood or supplies or game that had been shot at a distance from camp.

Craig MacDonald of Ontario has researched canoe hauling via sled in his region and has developed a sled specific to hauling canoes and composed of the minimum number of parts to do the job. There are two 7-foot runners shod with high-density plastic for maximum slip and two cross pieces, and the whole system is designed to come apart for more convenient stowage. The canoe is sledded upright with the load in it, and the take-down sled can literally be slid into the water from the ice along with the canoe. A lanyard can pull the sled up from beneath the canoe, a few lashings can be undone, and the four pieces can be packed until needed again.

Craig has led several "canoe" trips in winter in the Haliburton region of Ontario to perfect and test this system. His participants and others he has influenced have taken some fairly serious trips by adopting such methods, including one couple that snowshoed overland into the headwaters of the Nahanni River and continued the trip via paddle after the ice and the worst of the high water went out in the spring.

In addition to canoe sleds that are made for the purpose, it is also possible to hew runners out of available wood in the bush. On a trip where wintering over in timbered country is going to be part of the plan, a set of runners could be made while waiting for the ice to make up. Such runners would of course be unshod and would pull a bit harder, but they would still pull better than a full hull in the snow. You could also ice the runners with a mixture of moss and water the way Inuit sled drivers did if they didn't have ivory or bone shoes on their dogsleds.

If you are far enough south for White Birches to grow, one of the simplest emergency sleds can be made from any birch that forks into two fairly equal trunks that are straight for at least the length of the desired sled. The crotched trunk is cut about a foot below the split, and each leg of the split is cut 7 or 8 feet back. The two legs are then hewed to 2-inch widths vertically, and the bottoms are hewed so a rise occurs just before the crotch joins the main trunk. A foot or so back from the crotch, the legs, which become the runners, are thinned to perhaps an inch thick and are bent with boiling water until the runners are parallel and as straight as can be. A crosspiece at the shoulders of the bend ensures that the runners will be parallel. Once the bending is done and the runners tied off at the proper width for drying, permanent crosspieces can be made and mortised and lashed to the runners. If this is to be a canoe sled, then bunks that are hewed to accept the rounded hull of the canoe can be made either as part of the crosspieces or as additional crossmembers that will span the runners after the structural work is completed.

In spruce country you will not have a nice crotched tree that yields ready-made support, and you will have to make each runner separately. Sturdy crossmembers mortised and lashed will yield a sled of adequate stability, and in fact the lashings allow a certain amount of flexibility, which is useful in irregular terrain. To tighten lashings fully, a thin wedge can be carved and pounded under the lashings to reduce or eliminate any slack.

Use of a canoe sled presupposes that an ice hook is also along, and entry and exit of open water remain the same as for ice-hook-only technique. Once hard ice is gained, the canoe and load can be shifted to the sled. In approaching water, the canoe is set on the ice and loaded for standard ice-hook entry.

Should you be caught by the need for an ice hook and not have one, it is possible to use your axe. Although this is not very convenient due to handle length and the shape of the bit, it can be done. You will have to chip a deep enough pocket in the ice for each pull-point so that the axe does not slip out. In thin ice this is no problem since you can drive the head all the way through and hook the edge of the hole firmly.

With care and caution the most intimidating conditions between seasons can safely be encountered, thus vastly increasing your mobility while maintaining safety. At such seasons staying dry has everything to do with comfort.

My personal paddle is more than a finely sculpted precision tool. On each side of its flared grip is a quotation to make my dreams vivid and my horizons limitless.

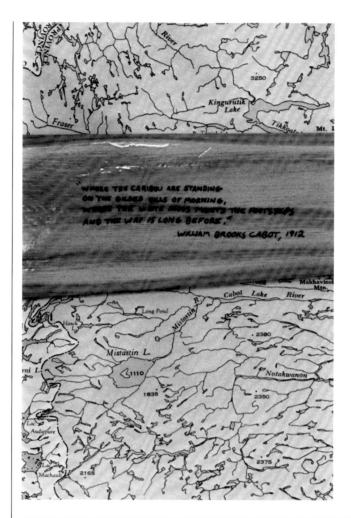

"WHERE THE CARIBOU ARE STANDING
ON THE GILDED HILLS OF MORNING,
WHERE THE WHITE MOSS PRINTS THE FOOTSTEPS
AND THE WAY IS LONG BEFORE."
WILLIAM BROOKS CABOT, 1912

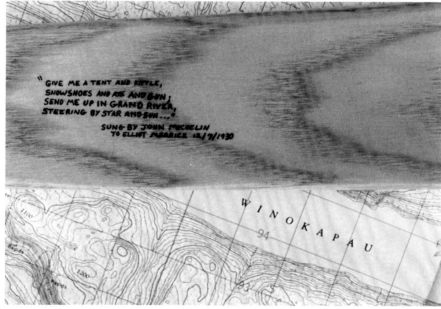

"GIVE ME A TENT AND KETTLE,
SNOWSHOES AND AXE AND GUN;
SEND ME UP IN GRAND RIVER,
STEERING BY STAR AND SUN..."
SUNG BY JOHN MICHELIN
TO ELLIOT MERRICK 12/7/1930

Afterword/Time, Judgment, and Process

Beyond the Paddle partially fills a niche that has been open in the existing literature about canoeing technique. It would be tempting to take more credit than this to fancy such a how-to manual as providing simple access to expertise, but by itself it cannot. At best it will provide a solid foundation from which understanding of the topics can grow, and serve as a stepping stone between the basics and actual practice in the field. As a learning tool it cannot provide the most necessary element of all, which is time—time for practice and perfection, for increasing the level of accomplishment, for advancing beyond the contents of the text. In this age of marketing, the implication that expertise is a commodity to be gained quickly through purchase of the right equipment or subscription to the right information is a myth wisely avoided.

Beyond the Paddle is best received as a ring of keys, with each key opening a door to a view of possibilities. It is up to all of us to open those doors and explore the view. Answers will come slowly and over time. With the passage of distance traveled, from the initial tens and hundreds of miles, to the accumulation of thousands, each measure of the way will yield the gifts that become our expertise and inform our judgment. The evolution and growth of an individual's judgment is a slow process that accumulates in each of us anecdotally, experimentally, and through trial and error. The trail must become the teacher and the student a shrewd and cautious observer.

My role has been as spokesperson with partial knowledge of some traditional skills that have application to the needs of the modern canoe voyageur. These skills have been refined over their long history through generations of native people, explorers, traders, and travelers. More recently some of them have left written or artistic records transferring an oral history and tradition of direct learning to those of us who must learn without benefit of being raised in the context of canoe travel, but who adopt it as recreation. Countless men and women have contributed to such knowledge and people like Francis Hopkins, Sigurd Olsen, Calvin Rutstrum, Heb Evans, C. E. S. Franks, Grace Lee Nute, Omer Stringer, and Bill Mason have each fanned the flames of these traditions, that those of us who have come later might learn. May each of us treat these flames with the same respect, add our own care as fuel, and pass both the heritage and our own discoveries to those who follow us.

Appendix/Striking a Waterline

There are two simple ways to strike a waterline on a canoe. Both will result in a perfectly serviceable line and, if done with care, will be neat and close to precise. For those who want a laser-perfect line, I recommend consulting a boat-building manual and reserving plenty of time for setting up and carrying out a vastly more complicated project.

Things will be easier if your canoe is symmetrical in sheer line because this will give you some measurable checkpoints to ascertain accuracy. All you need for the first method is a flat floor space large enough to accommodate your canoe.

Assuming this is available, you will need the following: a carpenter's level that can span the canoe (or a shorter level that can be put on a board that spans the canoe); a tape measure; a square; a few odd blocks of wood 1 to 2 inches thick; a pencil or marker that will show up on your hull material; a thin wooden batten at least 10 feet long and 1 inch wide; a self-sticking pinstripe from your local auto parts store in a color that contrasts with your canoe; and access to a cross-cut saw and a squared-off piece of wood such as the end of a plank.

Once the canoe is sitting on the floor in an upright position, check and see if it is sitting flat. In a canoe with a lot of rocker to the bottom, you may want to slip something like a 1-inch shim under each end the same distance from the cut-water of bow and stern. This will ensure that the canoe is flat relative to the

A restored canoe gets a waterline in the Northwoods Canoe Shop. With rails level and hull stabilized with wedges, Rollin Thurlow scribes a line.

floor. With the level across the rails (or on a board that spans the rails) or the center-thwart, get the canoe level laterally, that is, each rail the same height above the floor, assuming your floor is level. With a few spare blocks of wood or something like a bunched-up jacket, block the canoe up in this level position. This way when you move around and trip over the ends or bump the canoe, you won't have to relevel it.

This accomplished, decide where between rail and bottom you would like the line to appear on the side. Let's say 6 inches above the floor looks good. Retrieve the plank you have for the purpose and measure $5^7/_8$ inches from a perfectly squared end. Use a square to draw your line, then saw the piece of plank off so it is square. The $^1/_8$ inch that is missing just happens to approximate the thickness of a standard pencil from its side to the center of the graphite.

Now you need to remember to hold this piece of plank so that the $5^7/_8$-inch dimension is oriented toward the ceiling, or vertically. Hold the pencil flat on the top edge and by sliding the block and pencil along the floor while the pencil is in contact with the hull, transfer a line to the hull all around the canoe at a height of 6 inches from the floor. This won't work well on a shag carpet, so choose a hard floor.

This line will of course reflect any discontinuities in the floor such as nail heads that aren't flush, skewed sheets of plywood, or any hollows or rises that may be present. That is why you have a nice, long, clear batten that you got from a local woodworking firm or lumberyard. If you discover that the waterline on one side of your canoe reflects that 2-inch deep drain on your garage floor, all is not lost. You can do a couple of things. Repeat the process on a flatter section of floor, or if your batten is long enough, span that devious sag and average the line back to flatness.

When checking your line for straightness, squint along it from the ends of the canoe and look at it from the side. From the side you can hold up a ruler or something with a flat edge and sight over it to see if the line is parallel to the edge. Average all discontinuities of the line with the batten until satisfactory straightness is achieved. Check this by measuring from various points on the rail down to the line and see if there is consistency on each side of the canoe. With luck you will find everything close and fine. If it isn't, regard the discrepancy as a flag that something is amiss. Recheck lateral levelness and all other factors. Don't affix your line until the mystery is solved and corrected.

Although you can only see one side of the canoe at a time from shore or from another canoe, check to make sure the lines from opposite sides of the canoe join at the stem and stern. When they do, you have deprived critics from asking questions about things like mismatched lines. When all is set, apply the self-adhesive line, or if you will be painting on the line, the masking tape.

When you are done, your housemates will like you better if you clean up, put the furniture back where you found it, and get the canoe out of the living room without knocking over any antique lamps or sweeping Grandfather's first decoy off the mantle. Better yet, plan this project for when no one is home—and make sure they are gone long enough for you not only to complete the project but to complete all recovery and disguise tactics.

If you don't have access to a flat floor, or are forbidden using one by housemates not keen on disruption, there is a different method for waterlining. It is a bit more complicated but, compared to boat-yard techniques, still within

Detail of waterlining with block and pencil on a flat floor. The canoe is stabilized with wedges with the rails level.

the realm of simplicity.

You will need a lawn or other substrate that can have sawhorses set on it and a few stakes driven into it. A flat surface is best though it need not be level. You will need a patient assistant willing to be bossed around and easily amused by mishaps, repeated attempts, and all sorts of contingencies that are sure to arise. You will need two sawhorses; a carpenter's level that can span the canoe; a few long, thick dowels that can be pounded into the ground; a piece of string that is longer than your canoe; a 2- or 3-foot-long stick, dowel, or broom handle; a pencil; blocks of wood for stabilizing the canoe once it is leveled laterally; a tape measure; and a long wooden batten.

With the canoe sitting upright on the horses, level it laterally and block it into position. It need not be level fore and aft, so sloping or uneven ground is no problem.

Pound two long dowels into the ground, one at each end of the canoe, a little past each stem and off to the side just far enough so that a string stretched between them will just touch the side of the canoe at its widest spot in the center.

At the center thwart, measure down to the spot where you would like your waterline to be and make a mark at that point for future reference.

With your trusty tape measure, go to one end of the canoe and measure back from the tip of the deck an arbitrary distance, such as 1 foot. Place a light mark here and declare the point no longer arbitrary. Measure straight down the side from this point to another arbitrary point, say 22 inches. Make a mark there, thus making a meaningful though temporary point. Go to the far end of the canoe and perform the same sequence using the same figures, which are now critically important.

Your long-suffering assistant can now have something to do. Instruct him or her to tie the string to the upright dowels at each end of the canoe, stretching it tightly enough so there is no sag in the line. If the dowels fall over with this much tension on them, pound them in deeper or brace them.

Rally your puzzled assistant to your side at one of the dowels. You have your trusty level and another dowel or stick to serve as an upright brace to stabilize the level. Put the top surface of one end of the level on the spot you marked that was 22 inches below the rail. Your free hand, which is holding the upright, has been strategically placed just outboard of the string on the dowels, and you now guide the level to a position that reads level with one end still on the mark on the hull. When this point is found, clamp the level to the upright between your thumb and fingers. Adjust for precision and instruct your helper to move the string by sliding it up or down on the dowel so that it too is tangent to the top surface of the level. Perform this same feat at the far end of the string and recheck each end to make sure the string is still tangent to the top surface of the level at bow and stern. When it is, proceed to the center of the canoe.

Here you will find that your string is in one place and your center dot, where you want the waterline, in another. If the string is tangent to the canoe, measure the distance between the string and your mark. Don't forget this figure.

If your string is at a distance from the side of the canoe, use your level and upright to project the exact position of the string to the canoe. To accomplish this, position the level so the string is tangent to the top surface of the level; then raise the end of the level that is closest to the canoe until the bubble reads level. Your helper will then step back to make sure the string is not sagging or that your version of tangent is not lifting it. When all is level, your assistant will mark the spot on the side of the canoe where the top surface of the level touches. This mark should be positioned so it is vertically aligned above or below your waterline mark. You have just successfully projected the position of the center of the string to the center of the canoe. You will find that this feat of projection is something you are about to get quite proficient at due to repetition.

Measure the vertical distance from waterline mark to the point projected from the string. Do not forget this figure.

Now proceed to one end of the canoe and adjust the string up or down the exact distance that was revealed at the center. Do this at the other end also, and success will be revealed by the string now intersecting the center point perfectly. If there is a remaining difference at the center, adjust each end with the new figure, which will equal the distance required for correction. This done, you now have a string that is exactly opposite where the waterline will fall on the canoe.

Because the canoe tapers toward each end, the side to which you will project the line is at varying distances from the string. It is this convexity that prevents you from simply snapping a chalkline as you might on a flat surface and that has precipitated the need for such an elaborate setup.

At this point you want to refrain from bumping the canoe, knocking over your dowels, or moving anything you have set up so far. You may now dispense with any of the formerly arbitrary numbers chosen for reference points at each end of the canoe. Thinking back over what you have done will reveal that those numbers merely created a baseline from which you could accurately measure corrective distances to establish a new line—which is now perfectly straight and at the level you wish your waterline to appear. You are now ready to project that line from the string to the side of the canoe by using the bubble in the level as your constant reference point. Since this is a point of gravity, the flatness of the

Waterlined canoes emerging from the Northwoods Canoe Shop.

ground has no bearing on the project. All that matters now is that the canoe is laterally level and that the string is exactly parallel to where you want the line to fall on the hull.

Do the projection process every few feet along the length of the canoe. Each time you get the level tangent to the string and the bubble centered, your helper will step back to check for a dip or rise in the string, and observing none, will mark the spot where the top surface of the level touches the canoe. Nine or ten such reference points should suffice.

Before moving a thing, check all the points by stepping back and sighting across the string. If the string eclipses your pencil marks, you have been stunningly accurate. Chances are a few marks will show a fraction of an inch above or below the line. These should be projected again to correct them.

With one side completed, turn the canoe 180 degrees, being careful not to knock over your hard-earned string, and relevel it laterally and block it into a stable position. Mark your center point as on the first side, and adjust your line if need be so that the string intersects the center point and the points at each end, which can now be carried around each stem from the far side of the canoe. If all three points line up, you are ready to proceed and by now have gotten good at projecting the points with your level as dictated by the line.

Once all is checked and rechecked and deemed close enough, you are ready to connect the reference points on each side of the canoe using the batten for a straightedge. This done, you are finally ready to affix masking tape for a painted line or to roll out an adhesive-backed pinstripe along your well-deserved reference line.

One trip on the water and the joys of achieving proper trim quickly and easily will more than compensate for the troubles and tribulations you incurred in striking the line. And if for some reason you know you want a waterline but have not yet ordered a canoe, and if your tendencies favor a wood and canvas canoe, then you are in luck. Many of the builders offer a paint and shellac waterline as an option. And who knows, with enough demand, maybe the manufacturers of synthetic canoes would produce waterlined canoes.